Grizzlies
Glaciers
and
Gourmet

By Alaskan Chef and Artist
Janet C Hickok

This is a Doriolas Publication

Copyright © 2004 by Janet C Hickok
All Rights Reserved

First Edition   September, 2004   5,000 Copies

ISBN 0-9760019-051500
Grizzlies Glaciers and Gourmet
Collection by Alaskan Chef Janet C Hickok

Book Design, Art Work and
Recipe Collection   - Janet C Hickok
Assistant and Technical Director - Duane O Hickok

Contributing Photographers - Bill Sims
                            Chad Whitcomb
                            Robert Hawkins
                            Louis Weber
                            Duane Hickok
                            Janet Hickok
All Art Work Copyright © of Artist 2004

Printed in ALASKA by
        AT Publishing
        1720 Abbott Road
        Anchorage, AK 99507

MADE IN ALASKA
No. 5567

Additional Copies of Grizzlies Glaciers and
Gourmet may be obtained by sending $20.00 plus $5
postage and handling to: Janet Hickok
                            PO Box 141539
                            Anchorage, AK
                            99514-1935

or online at : www.doriolas.com

Dedication

To my unbelievably WON-derful parents, Paul and Doris, with all my thanks for giving and teaching unconditional and unending love.
To Nancy, Susan, David, Vivian, Joyce, Karen, and Duane - my bodacious siblings and best friends.

Acknowledgments

A huge thank you to Nonie Turville, without whom (as "cliché" as it may sound) this book would not exist. Also, a hefty thank you to Jason Roth. Both had faith in a dream that wasn't theirs and showed true friendship.

A GIANT thanks to Duane, for the countless hours, unending energy and much-needed technical support and advice - generously given at all times - without reservation or grudging, and to Kylee for never complaining when he did so. Viv, your hours of help were invaluable and greatly appreciated.

I am supremely grateful to Bill Sims, who allowed me the opportunity and means of experiencing the Alaska you see in this book, and for employing me through the years in the best job a person could ever hope for. Thanks to Sharon Sims for kindness and caring that inspired and sustained me. You two are family!

Rogene, your help came at a crucial time and is extremely appreciated. Thanks to all the contributing photographers for sharing your art. Lastly, thanks to the many wonderful folks who have visited Newhalen Lodge year after year and shared their recipes. I truly appreciate all who have contributed to this book.

These are only a small portion of the recipes that I have used over the years at Newhalen Lodge. There are, of course, many, many more. Having had no professional training, I learned to cook from my mother and sisters. I gleaned culinary knowledge from books, magazines, cooking shows, on-the-job training and fellow gastronomic artists. Many recipes credited to me may be similar to others you have tasted or seen. This is due, I believe, to the fact that the best recipes are repetitions - with individual twists that return to enchant the taste buds time and again. I learn new recipes and ideas weekly and continue to build my repertoire, so be on the lookout for my next cookbook!

Appetizers

Ten Layer Tortilla Pie

Janet Hickok
Servings 16

3	cans black beans -- rinsed and drained
1	can black olives -- drained and halved
16	ounces green chiles - diced
1	cup cilantro - chopped
2	whole tomatoes -- diced small
3	cups cheddar cheese - shredded
4	whole green onions - diced
10	flour tortillas
	Sour cream -- for accompaniment, optional
	Salsa -- for accompaniment, optional

Prepare all ingredients ahead of time. Assemble just before baking.

Start with one tortilla and place in a greased pie pan. Layer ingredients in any order that you like. The plan is very simple and easy. I find that placing a small amount of cheese on each, or every other layer works the best and acts as a type of "glue" to hold the entire thing together. Remember to leave a small amount of cheese, tomato and green onion for the top to garnish. Continue layering until all ingredients are used.

Bake at 350 degrees for 20-30 minutes. Be sure to heat through completely. If the top is getting too dark, gently lay a sheet of foil to shield it until done.

Let set for 15-20 minutes before cutting. Serve with a side of salsa and sour cream if desired.

NOTE: This recipe can be split between two pie plates, which makes a five layer pie and less time to heat through. Feel free to add or subtract ingredients to your taste. I have used refried beans to add more body and like canned or pickled jalapenos. Chicken, cut or finely shredded, adds a nice touch.

Anytime Pesto-Pizza Bagels

Janet Hickok
Servings 12

6	bagels -- halved
12	ounces cream cheese -- softened
1/3	cup pesto sauce -- preferably fresh
3	whole tomatoes -- thinly sliced
1	cup parmesan cheese -- grated
12	Canadian bacon slices -- optional

Toast the bagel halves and cool completely; set aside. Cover tightly with plastic wrap until needed.

Place the sliced tomatoes on several layers of paper towel and sprinkle with salt. Let set for 1-2 hours to intensify flavor and drain.

Whip together the cream cheese and pesto until well combined.

Preheat the broiler. Adjust rack to center of oven.

Begin to assemble by smearing each bagel half with the cream cheese-pesto mix and topping with Canadian bacon, if using. Top with one or two slices of tomato and then sprinkle generously with parmesan cheese.

Broil until slightly brown and cheese is bubbling. Remove and let set for a couple of minutes. Serve as halves or cut into smaller, bite-size pieces.

NOTE: These are super delicious and can be used for breakfast, for lunch with a salad, for appetizers, or as a filling snack. I have used prosciutto, thinly-sliced deli ham, and even crisp cooked bacon, as an alternative to the Canadian bacon. It is also fantastic without meat as a vegetarian treat.

Jimmy Jack's Shrimp Cocktail

Mary Ann Houtz
Servings: 16

2	cups clam and tomato juice blend
1	cup fresh orange juice
1	cup V-8® vegetable juice
2	small limes -- juiced
2	tablespoons red wine vinegar
1/2	cup ketchup
1	tablespoon worcestershire sauce
1	tablespoon soy sauce
1/4	teaspoon garlic salt -- or to taste
1/4	teaspoon celery salt -- or to taste
1/4	teaspoon cayenne pepper -- or to taste
1/4	teaspoon black pepper -- or to taste
1/2	teaspoon chili powder
1	bunch green onion -- chopped
1/4	cup finely chopped basil
1/2	cup parsley -- chopped
1/2	cup cilantro -- chopped
2	medium avocados -- cubed
2	pounds cooked shrimp -- peeled and deveined

Combine juices, vinegar, ketchup, worcestershire sauce, soy, seasonings, and onion; stir well.

Just before serving, add fresh herbs, avocados and shrimp, folding to incorporate. Chill.
Serve with saltine crackers in the style of Mexican shrimp, cocktails or with your choice of crackers or chips.

Artichoke~Jalapeno Dip

Janet Hickok
Servings 48

62	ounces marinated artichoke hearts -- drained and coarsely chopped
3	cups mayonnaise
1 1/2	cups parmesan cheese -- grated
1 1/2	cups mozzarella cheese -- shredded
2	jalapenos -- minced
1	tablespoon toasted sesame seeds -- optional
1	teaspoon fresh ground black pepper -- optional

Preheat oven to 350 degrees.

Blend artichoke hearts, mayonnaise and cheeses together in a large bowl. When well mixed, place as much as you'd like of the dip in a baking dish and top with sesame seeds or cracked pepper.

Bake 30 minutes or until browned and bubbly. Let set for 10 minutes and then serve with assorted crackers or toasted French bread slices.

This recipe makes a lot. Store remainder of the mix in tightly sealed container in the fridge for up to 3 weeks.

NOTE: This is so easy to whip up if company arrives, and convenient to keep on hand. It is also great with crab, shrimp or chicken added to bulk it up and make it a heartier dish.

Wildfire Chili-Cheese Dip

Charlynn Casey
Servings 18

1	cup	mayonnaise
3	ounces	parmesan cheese -- grated
12	ounces	monterey jack cheese -- grated
9	ounces	green chiles -- chopped
22	ounces	canned corn -- mexican style
4	ounces	pimientos -- chopped

Preheat oven to 350 degrees.

Mix all ingredients together until well blended and turn out into a 2 quart baking dish. Bake for 30-40 minutes or until slightly browned. Serve with choice of crackers or bread.

Casey's Crab Dip

Louis Casey
Servings 12

6 1/2	ounces	crab meat
4		eggs, hard-boiled
2 1/2	cups	soft bread crumbs -- plus 1 cup more
1	cup	parmesan cheese
3	tablespoons	parsley -- chopped
2	tablespoons	green pepper -- minced
3	tablespoons	green onion -- minced
3	tablespoons	lemon juice
1	pinch	onion salt -- or to taste
1	pinch	garlic powder -- or to taste
1	can	cream of mushroom soup
1	cup	mayonnaise
1/2	cup	half and half
2	teaspoons	mustard

Combine 1 cup of the bread crumbs and the parmesan cheese and set aside. Mix all other ingredients very well and turn into a low, shallow baking dish. Salt and pepper to taste. Spread the reserved cheese and bread crumbs on top. Can be prepared up to one day ahead.
Bake at 400 degrees for 15-20 minutes.

Pico De Gallo Festivo

Janet Hickok
Servings 8

4	tablespoons onions -- diced
4	cups tomatoes -- cut in 1/4-inch cubes
1	yellow bell pepper -- diced small
4	serrano peppers -- seeded, finely minced
4	tablespoons cilantro -- finely chopped
2	teaspoons sugar -- or to taste
4	teaspoons Kosher or sea salt -- or to taste
1	lime -- juice of

Put diced onion in a large bowl, and cover with 1 cup of boiling water. Let set for 2 minutes, drain very well. Combine all the remaining ingredients with the onions and mix well. Let sit in the fridge for at least 30 minutes before serving.

Di Weber's Goat Cheese-Pecan Dip

Diane Weber
Servings 8

8	ounces goat cheese -- softened
8	ounces cream cheese -- softened
1	tablespoon garlic -- minced
3	tablespoons fresh basil -- chopped
3/4	cup pecans -- caramelized or candied
1/4	cup olive oil -- or as needed

Preheat oven to 350 degrees.

Combine goat and cream cheeses. You may use just goat cheese if you'd like. Spread in a baking dish and layer on garlic and basil. Chop up pecans and sprinkle on top, drizzle with olive oil and place in oven for 10-12 minutes or until heated through. Serve with assorted crackers, bagel chips or lavosh.

Goat Cheese Quesadillas With Roasted Red Pepper Sauce

Tani Sanchez
Servings 4

1/2	cup onions -- chopped fine
3	cloves garlic -- minced
2	red bell peppers -- roasted and peeled
2	tablespoons fresh basil -- chopped
6	flour tortillas
4	ounces goat cheese -- soft
1/2	cup basil pesto
2	tablespoons butter -- soft

SAUCE: Cook onion and garlic with 1 tablespoon olive oil over medium heat until soft. Transfer to a food processor and add peppers, basil, salt and pepper to taste.
Spread a tortilla with 1 1/2 tablespoons of goat cheese; top with 1 tablespoon pesto. Repeat to make another layer and top with plain tortilla. Fry in butter over med-high heat until both sides are golden. Serve immediately with Red Pepper Sauce.

Cheesy Shrimp Dip

Tracey Drummond
Servings 8

6	ounces small shrimp -- cooked
8	ounces cheddar cheese -- shredded
1/2	small onion -- chopped fine
1	cup mayonnaise
1	tablespoon worcestershire sauce
1	pinch garlic salt -- or to taste

Mix all ingredients together until smooth and well blended. Chill overnight in fridge for best results.

Serve with choice of crackers, vegetables or toasts.

Alaska "Gold" Salmon Nuggets

Janet Hickok
Servings 20

1 1/2	cups canned or cooked fresh salmon
1/2	cup mashed potatoes
1	teaspoon fresh or 1/2 teaspoon dried dill
1/2	teaspoon honey
1	teaspoon worcestershire sauce
1	tablespoon celery -- minced fine
1	tablespoon onion -- minced fine
1	tablespoon butter
	Kosher or sea salt -- to taste
	pepper -- to taste
1/2	pound cheddar cheese -- cut into 1/2" cubes
2	eggs -- beaten
1 1/2	cups panko -- or flour or cracker crumbs

Mix salmon, potatoes, dill, lemon juice, honey, and worcestershire sauce.

Melt butter in a medium size skillet and cook celery and onion until tender; mix with salmon. Add salt and pepper and shape into balls or patties. Push a cube of cheese into center. Dip each into egg and then roll in crumbs or flour.

Fry at 375 degrees until golden brown. Drain and serve.

Roast Garlic and Cambozola Pita Triangles

Janet Hickok
Servings 6

1/2	**cup roasted garlic**
1	**tablespoon olive oil**
1	**pound cambozola cheese -- room temperature**
1/8	**teaspoon Kosher or sea salt**
1/4	**teaspoon fresh ground black pepper**
2	**whole green onions -- minced**
1	**pinch sugar**

Coarsely mash together all ingredients until uniformly mixed.
Serve with soft, fresh pita triangles or other soft bread.

Shrimp or Scallop Bacon Wrapped Bundles

Janet Hickok
Servings 15

1	**pound shrimp or scallops, peeled and deveined**
4	**cups boiling, salted water**
1/2	**pound bacon -- sliced**
1	**clove garlic -- minced**
1/2	**cup Pridgen's Cocktail Sauce -- See page 105**

Cook shrimp in boiling water until they just start to turn pink, about
3 minutes. Drain, cool. (No need to pre-cook scallops.)
Cook bacon strips until just limp and pliable. Drain; cut in half.
Stir together garlic and cocktail sauce. Dip each shrimp or
scallop in sauce and then wrap with a half piece of bacon,
securing with a toothpick.
May be covered and chilled until next day up to this point.
To cook, place on a sheet pan and broil, turning once, or grill on
high until bacon is crisp and browned. Serve hot.

Breads and
Breakfasts

Suzie's Tender Cornmeal Buns

Susan Hickok
Makes 2 Dozen Medium Sized

1/3	cup yellow cornmeal, whole grain
1/2	cup sugar
2	teaspoons salt
1/2	cup butter
1	cup milk
2	cups water
2	packages yeast
1/4	cup warm water
1	teaspoon sugar
2	whole eggs
4	cups flour

Combine the first 6 ingredients in a saucepan and cook on medium-high heat until the consistency of cooked cereal. Remove from heat. Place a piece of plastic wrap directly on the surface of the cooked cornmeal and set aside to cool until luke-warm.

Combine yeast, water, and sugar and let set for 10 minutes, or until foamy.

Add yeast mix to cornmeal mix and stir to combine. Add eggs and 4 or more cups of flour (dough should be very soft and slightly sticky). Knead well. Let rise for about 60 minutes or until almost doubled in size. Punch down and roll out to 1/2 inch thick. Cut with biscuit cutter and place on greased pans. Cover and let rise once more, in a warm place, until doubled in size.

Preheat oven to 375 degrees. Place buns in oven and bake for 15 minutes.

NOTE: Dough keeps well in refrigerator for up to four days. Buns freeze well after baking.

Bodacious Banana Bread

Aunt Lucille LiaBraaten
Makes 1 Loaf

1	cup sugar
1/2	cup shortening
2	large eggs
3	small bananas -- mashed
1	teaspoon soda
2	cups flour
3	tablespoons buttermilk -- or 3 tablespoons milk with 1 teaspoon vinegar
1/2	teaspoon salt
1	teaspoon vanilla
1	cup walnuts -- chopped

Preheat oven to 350 degrees.

Cream sugar and shortening together until well mixed. Add eggs and mix. Stir in mashed bananas and mix until combined. Add dry ingredients alternately with buttermilk or sour milk - *See Note. Start and end with dry indredients. Fold in nuts and vanilla. Pour into loaf pan.

Bake for 50-60 minutes or until pick inserted in center comes out clean. Leave in pan for 15 minutes, turn out of pan onto a wire rack and cool.

*NOTE: The original recipe calls for sour milk, which is the milk/ vinegar combination. I have also used sour cream and had success.

Tortillas de Harina

Natalia, Laredo, Texas
Makes Approximately 2 Dozen

4	cups all-purpose flour
2	teaspoons salt
1 1/2	teaspoons baking powder
1	cup vegetable shortening
1	cup hot water

Combine all but the water in a large bowl and work with hands until a fine crumb is formed.

Add the hot water and knead until very smooth and soft. Form into small, even discs. Let rest 10-15 minutes.

I was taught by Natalia to roll out the dough without turning over, until thin and evenly flat and then cook over medium-high heat on a comal or griddle until slightly browned, flipping them over exactly three times in the process. Cook through until the doughy translucency is gone, they are covered with brown spots, and the tortillas are soft and tender. Tortillas will puff up into balloons during the cooking process if done correctly.

NOTE: This recipe makes enough tortillas to freeze. If you are not going to eat them immediately, it is much better to cook the tortillas half way and then finish the cooking process when they are re-heated for later use. Cool and then stack with wax or parchment paper between tortillas. Freeze in a zip top plastic bag until ready to use. Reheat over medium heat.

Pozzi Beer Bread

Bruce and Susan Pozzi
Makes 1 Loaf

3	**cups flour**
4 1/2	**teaspoons baking powder**
1 1/2	**teaspoons salt**
3	**tablespoons sugar**
1	**can beer -- room temperature**
1/4	**cup butter -- melted**

Preheat oven to 350 degrees.

Mix all but the butter and pour into a well-greased bread pan. Pour melted butter immediately on top of batter and bake for 50 minutes.

Broccoli Maizecake

James Wright
Serves 12

4	**whole eggs -- blended**
1	**mediun onion -- diced fine**
10	**ounces broccoli, frozen -- chopped, thawed**
1	**stick butter -- melted**
1/2	**stick butter**
5	**cups cornbread mix**

Preheat oven to 350 degrees. Drain broccoli extremely well.

Mix melted butter, eggs, onion, broccoli, and cornbread together in large bowl; batter will be very thick. Put the remaining 1/2 stick of butter in a 9X13-inch glass pan and place in the oven just until butter melts. Immediately pour batter into pan and spread evenly.
Bake 30-45 minutes or until toothpick inserted in center of cornbread comes out clean. Let set for 10 minutes and then cut into squares and serve hot.

Sausage Gravy

Janet Hickok
Servings 10

1	pound sausage -- your favorite
1/4	cup flour
1	teaspoon Kosher or sea salt -- or to taste
1/2	teaspoon fresh ground black pepper -- or to taste
4	cups milk -- or more if needed. I use cream and milk

Cut up sausage chub/roll into slices. Using 2 slices, fry in a heavy saucepan over medium heat until crumbled and browned, stirring to break up and cook evenly.

Add the flour, salt and pepper and let cook, stirring often until flour is scorched and turning tan-ish. Whisk in milk and continue to cook until thickened and bubbly. Add more milk or cream if desired, to make the gravy as thick or thin as you prefer. Stir frequently. Adjust seasonings.

Mom's Morning Biscuits

Doris Hickok
Makes 1 dozen

3 1/4	cups flour
2	tablespoons baking powder
1 1/2	teaspoon Kosher salt
8	tablespoons cold butter, cut into pieces
1	cup milk, plus 2 tablespoons

Preheat oven to 450 degrees.
Stir together all the dry ingredients. With a pastry blender, cut in the shortening and then the cold water. Handling as little as possible, form into a soft dough. Roll out to 1/2 inch thick and cut into biscuits. Bake for 12-15 minutes.

Parmesan Bread

Kylee Hickok
Makes 1 Large Loaf

1	package yeast
1	cup warm water
3	cups flour
1/4	cup butter
1	beaten egg
2	tablespoons sugar
1	teaspoon salt
1	teaspoon dried onion flakes
1/2	teaspoon Italian seasoning
1/2	cup freshly grated parmesan cheese -- or canned dried

Preheat oven to 350 degrees.

In large mixer bowl, dissolve yeast in water. Let set for 10 minutes. Add 2 cups of the flour, butter, egg, sugar, salt and seasonings. Beat at low for 2 minutes, stir in remaining flour and 1/4 cup of the cheese. Turn out into a greased bowl. Let rise for 1 hour in a warm place until doubled.
Knead for 2 minutes. Place in greased round, oven-proof bowl (1 1/2 qt) and let raise again for 30 minutes.
Bake for 35 minutes.

Note: I found it works better to cook for half the time and then brush with melted butter and sprinkle with remaining cheese and return to oven to finish cooking.

Monday's Sticky Buns

Janet Hickok
Servings 48

1	1/4 ounce package yeast
1	tablespoon sugar
1	cup warm water
10	cups all-purpose flour
2	tablespoons salt
1	stick butter -- softened
1/2	cup sugar
3	cups cold water
1 1/2	cups brown sugar
1	cup light corn syrup
6	tablespoons butter -- melted
6	tablespoons cinnamon -- or more if needed

Combine yeast and sugar in a two cup measuring cup with the warm water (110 degrees).

Let set until yeast activates and is foamy, about 10 minutes. When yeast is ready, combine with the 3 cups cold water.

In a food processor fitted with the dough blade, pulse the flour, salt, butter and sugar. Then, with processor running, slowly pour in the water/yeast mix through the feeder tube and let mix until a dough ball is formed (you may only need 2 1/2 -2 3/4 cup of water). Let mix for 90 seconds for the kneading process.
Turn out into a greased bowl and cover with plastic. Place in a warm place and let rise until doubled in bulk. About 45-60 minutes.

Preheat oven to 375 degrees. Generously grease three 9x13 inch glass baking dishes. In each of the dishes, spread 1/3 of the brown sugar, and drizzle with 1/3 of the corn syrup and 2 table-spoons melted butter. Set aside.
Roll out one third of the dough and sprinkle with cinnamon to taste. Roll up in a long cigar shape and cut into about 1 1/4 inch

pieces. Repeat with remaining dough.

Place rolls, cut side down, in the prepared pans, cover with plastic and let rise until doubled, about 35-45 minutes. Bake for 30 minutes. Rotate pans top to bottom half way through the cooking time.

NOTE: This can be halved for smaller processors or for standing, electric mixers. If using an electric mixer, you will need to use the dough hook, and let the dough mix on low for 10 minutes for the kneading step.

Blueberry Buckle Coffeecake

Rhonda Seline
Serves 15

3	cups flour
1	cup sugar
2	teaspoons baking powder
1	teaspoon salt
1	cup milk
1 1/2	cups blueberries -- fresh or frozen
1/2	cup flour
2/3	cup brown sugar
1	teaspoon cinnamon
6	tablespoons firm butter -- cut into pieces

Preheat oven to 375 degrees. Generously butter and flour a 9x13-inch baking pan.

In an electric mixing bowl, set on low speed, gently stir first five ingredients together until just mixed and all is moist. Remove bowl from mixer and carefully fold in blueberries.
Turn batter out into prepared pan.
Combine remaining ingredients and mix on medium speed until crumbly. Sprinkle evenly on top of batter. Place in oven and bake for 30-35 minutes or until toothpick inserted in center of cake comes out clean. Let cool in pan, on a wire rack for at least 20 minutes before cutting and serving.

Quiche Real Men Will Eat

Janet Hickok

1	pie crust (9 inch) bought, pre-made
8	ounces bacon -- cut into bits
4	large egg yolks
1	cup half and half
1	cup whipping cream
1/2	teaspoon salt
1/2	teaspoon white pepper
1	pinch sugar
1	teaspoon herbs -- your choice
4	ounces Swiss cheese -- grated (or Gruyere cheese)

Adjust oven rack to center position and heat oven to 375 degrees. Pierce the pre-made pie shell all over with a fork and bake for 12 minutes while preparing remainder of ingredients.

Fry bacon until crisp and brown, about 10 minutes. Drain well.

Meanwhile, whisk all remaining ingredients except cheese in medium bowl.

Spread cheese and bacon evenly over bottom of warm pie shell. Carefully pour custard mix to 1/2 inch below crust rim. Bake until lightly golden brown and a knife inserted in center comes out clean, and quiche feels set but soft like gelatin, about 35 minutes. Cool on a rack. Serve warm or at room temperature.

NOTE: This is the basic quiche recipe that can be used for any kind of ingredients that you prefer. I like this with ham bits, sausage, canadian bacon, prosciutto, tomatoes, zucchini, mushrooms, onions, fresh spinach, etc., etc.

Breads and Breakfasts

Apricot Empanadas

Yvonne in Laredo
Servings 24

8	ounces cream cheese
1	cup butter
1	tablespoon sour cream
2 1/2	cups flour
1	pinch salt
1/4	cup powdered sugar

Beat cream cheese with butter and sour cream until smooth.
Slowly add flour, salt and sugar. Form a ball and chill for an hour.
Roll out dough and cut with a cookie cutter. Fill with 1 tablespoon
of your choice of fillings (use jams or pie fillings). Seal edges with
water and press with a fork. Apply egg wash (I spray with nonstick
oil spray) and sprinkle with small amount of granulated sugar
before baking. Chill for 30 minutes.
Meanwhile, preheat oven to 375 degrees.
Bake for 15-20 minutes or until lightly browned.

Angelfire Eggs

Mary Ann Houtz
Servings 20

1	tablespoon unsalted butter
2	cups fresh mushrooms -- thinly sliced
2	cans mushroom soup, condensed
2	dozen eggs -- lightly beaten
1/2	cup sherry
1/2	pound grated cheese -- your choice
1	cup bread crumbs

In a large skillet, melt the butter and saute the mushrooms until
softened and slightly browned. Cool. In a large mixing bowl,
place the eggs and soup concentrate. Whisk until thoroughly
combined. Stir in the remaining ingredients and pour into a 9x13-
inch dish, or divide between two dishes. Cover and chill overnight.

Preheat oven to 350 degrees. Sprinkle top with bread crumbs and
bake until bubbly and the eggs are just set, approximately 35
minutes

Gold Rush Sourdough Starter

Doris Hickok
Servings Unlimited

SOURDOUGH
4	medium potatoes - cubed, (2 cups)
2	cups rye flour
2	cups all-purpose flour
2	teaspoons salt
1/2	cup honey

SPONGE/STARTER
2	cups water -- warm
2 1/2	cups all-purpose flour

PANCAKES
1	egg
2	tablespoons oil
1/4	cup evaporated milk
1	teaspoon soda
1	teaspoon salt
2	tablespoons sugar

Wash and peel potatoes, cube and boil in 4 cups of water, reserving 3 cups of potato water after boiling. Drain potatoes and mash well.

Combine 3 cups of potato water, both flours, salt, and honey. Mix well. Cover bowl and leave at room temperature for 4 days.

Sour dough is now ready to use in recipes. Store in glass jar in fridge. Remember to replenish your supply from the flour and water sponge that is mixed the night before you want to make a recipe. Return back to jar in preparation for next time.

SOURDOUGH SPONGE/STARTER:
Evening Before: Add warm water and flour to 1 cup of the sourdough starter to make a sponge. Beat well, cover, and let set in warm place overnight.

SOURDOUGH PANCAKES:

Next Morning - remove one cup of sponge/starter and return to supply stored in the fridge. To the remaining sponge, add egg, oil and evaporated milk, mix well. Beat in soda, salt and sugar. Cook as you would any other type of pancakes.

Sourdough Bread

Doris Hickok
Yield 2 loaves

1	cup sourdough starter sponge
1	1/4 ounce package yeast
1 1/2	cups warm water
6	cups flour
2	tablespoons sugar
1/2	teaspoon soda
1/2	teaspoon salt

Keep 1 cup of the prepared sourdough starter sponge from the previous recipe and put back in the fridge for the next time. Use the remainder for this recipe.

Add yeast to warm water (105-110 degrees). When foamy, add in the sourdough sponge, 4 cups of the flour, sugar and salt. Beat well. Place in a greased bowl and let rise until doubled.
Dough will be a very soft.
Stir soda into 1 cup of the flour and add to the doubled dough. Knead gently until dough is satiny and springy to the touch, using the extra cup of flour on kneading surface as necessary. Let rest for 15-20 minutes and then form into 2 loaves and place in greased pans. Let rise again.

Preheat oven to 400 degrees and bake for 35-40 minutes.

Nanny's Whipped Cream Biscuits with Cranberry-Orange Butter

Merrie French's Grandmother, 1956
Servings 24

3	cups sifted all purpose flour
1 1/2	teaspoons Kosher salt
8	teaspoons baking powder
2	cups heavy cream -- whipped
1/2	cup melted butter

Preheat oven to 450 degrees. Butter a 9x13 inch baking dish; set aside.

Place dry ingredients in a large bowl. Blend in the whipped cream with a fork until stiff dough forms. Turn onto a floured board and knead slightly. Roll to 1/2" thick and cut into 2-inch rounds with a biscuit cutter. Arrange biscuits in prepared pan with sides touching. Brush tops with melted butter.

Bake until golden - approximately 20-25 minutes.

BUTTER: Beat 1 cup of butter until fluffy. Add 1/3 cup of whole Berry Cranberry Sauce and 2 tablespoons of Orange Marmalade and beat until well mixed.
Can be kept in fridge for up to 3 weeks.

Spudnuts

Doris Hickok from Betty Stier
Servings 24

1	1/4 ounce package yeast
1	teaspoon sugar
1/2	cup warm water, 110-112 degrees
1	cup mashed potatoes
1/4	cup sugar
1/2	teaspoon soda
1	teaspoon salt
2	whole eggs
1 1/2	cups milk
1/3	cup butter -- melted
6	cups flour, or as needed
2	cups powdered sugar
2	tablespoons cornstarch
2	tablespoons warm milk -- or more if needed

In a large mixing bowl dissolve yeast and sugar in warm water and let set for 10 minutes to allow yeast to activate.

Add potatoes, sugar, soda, salt, eggs, milk, and butter. Stir to combine. Add in half of the flour and mix well. Knead in rest of flour or when dough is just dry and firm enough to handle. Dough will be very soft and should be handled as little as possible. Roll out to 1/2 inch thick on a generously floured surface and cut out with donut cutter. Let set for 15 minutes. Pull holes with fingers before frying.

Deep fry in 375 degree vegetable oil. Flip donuts when golden brown on one side, cook until golden on other side. Drain on paper towels or brown paper sacks.

GLAZE: Whisk together the powdered sugar, cornstarch and milk to a consistency you prefer. Drizzle or pour over warm donuts and let set on rack for 20 minutes.

New York Minute Crumb Cake

Janet Hickok
Servings 20

3	cups all-purpose flour
1	cup sugar
5	teaspoons baking powder
1	teaspoon Kosher or sea salt
2	large eggs
1	cup milk
4	tablespoons canola oil
4	teaspoons vanilla
2 1/2	cups all-purpose flour
1	cup brown sugar
1 1/2	teaspoons cinnamon
2	sticks cold butter -- cut into pieces

Preheat oven to 325 degrees. Grease a 9x13 inch glass baking dish.

Mix the first 4 dry ingredients well, set aside.

Whisk the next 4 ingredients together and add the dry ingredients, mixing and stirring to combine evenly. Turn out batter into the prepared pan.

Mix flour, sugar, and cinnamon together; crumble the butter into this mixture until it resembles coarse meal. Sprinkle evenly on top of the batter.

Bake for 20-25 minutes or until lightly browned and just cooked through. Cool on rack for 12 minutes. Dust heavily with powdered sugar before serving.

Aunt Cherry's Oatmeal Coffee Cake

Merrie French
Servings 16

1	cup oatmeal
1	cup sugar
1	cup brown sugar
1 1/3	cups flour
1/2	teaspoon Kosher salt
1	teaspoon baking soda
1	teaspoon cinnamon
1	teaspoon nutmeg
2	large eggs
1/2	cup melted butter
1 1/2	cups boiling water
1	cup chopped nuts
1/2	cup brown sugar
1/2	cup sugar
1/4	cup cream
6	tablespoons melted butter
1	cup shredded coconut meat
1	teaspoon vanilla

Preheat oven to 350 degrees. Butter and flour a 9x13 inch pan.

In a large bowl, mix the oatmeal and sugars. Sift together the flour, salt, soda, cinnamon and nutmeg and add to the sugar mix. Carefully whisk eggs, melted butter and boiling water. Fold into the dry ingredients mixture. Pour batter out into prepared pan.

Combine the nuts, sugars, cream, melted butter, coconut and vanilla and drop by small spoonfuls evernly over unbaked cake batter.

Bake for 45 minutes.

Sausage and Egg Casserole

Mary Ann Houtz
Servings 18

1	pound sausage meat -- cooked, crumbled and drained
1/2	teaspoon seasoned salt
8	large eggs -- beaten
2	cups milk
2	tablespoons yellow mustard
1/4	teaspoon Kosher or sea salt
1	pinch fresh ground black pepper
6	slices white bread -- cubed
2	tablespoons onion -- minced
1	cup cheddar cheese -- grated

Cook sausage in a medium skillet over medium heat, sprinkling with the seasoned salt. Drain thoroughly on paper towels. In a large mixing bowl whisk eggs with the mustard, milk, salt, pepper, and cooked sausage.

In a greased 9x13-inch baking dish, place the bread cubes and the sausage, spreading evenly. Carefully pour the egg mix over the top. Sprinkle the cheese evenly over the top. Cover and chill overnight.

Preheat oven to 350 degrees. Let casserole come to room temperature. Bake for 35-40 minutes.

30

34

Soups

Beefy Bean-Pot Soup

Janet Hickok
Servings 8

1	tablespoon olive oil
2	pounds lean ground beef
1	tablespoon olive oil
1	cup onions -- chopped
1	cup celery -- chopped
1	cup carrots -- chopped
1	clove garlic -- minced
4	cups beef broth
1	cup potato -- cut in 1/2" pieces
8	ounces canned tomatoes -- diced
1	cup frozen broccoli flowerets
1	cup frozen corn kernels
1/2	cup frozen peas
2	cans cannelini beans -- or your favorite
1 1/2	teaspoons sugar
1/2	teaspoon fresh thyme -- or to taste
1/4	teaspoon oregano
1/4	cup fresh parsley -- chopped
	Kosher or sea salt and fresh ground black pepper -- to taste

Add olive oil to heavy, large stockpot and brown the hamburger over medium-high heat. Remove from pan, drain and set aside.

Add olive oil to stockpot and saute onion for 5 minutes, or until beginning to soften. Add celery and cook another 2 minutes. Add the carrots, garlic and saute for another minute. Add beef broth, potatoes, tomatoes and bring to a boil. Reduce heat to low and simmer for 20 minutes. Add frozen vegetables, beans, sugar, and herbs. Simmer for another 30-40 minutes or until the vegetables are soft and cooked through. Season to taste with salt and pepper.

Cream of Wild Rice Soup

Janet Hickok
Servings 16

1	pound bacon -- or more if desired
1	large onion -- diced
4	stalks celery -- diced
2	teaspoons garlic -- minced
6	cups chicken stock
2	cups wild rice
1 1/2	teaspoons brown sugar
1	teaspoon fresh thyme -- minced
1/2	teaspoon fresh rosemary -- minced fine
4	cups heavy cream -- or more if needed
	Kosher or sea salt and fresh ground black pepper -- to taste
2	tablespoons cornstarch
3	tablespoons cold water

In a large stock pot, cook bacon until crisp and brown; remove bacon from the grease. Drain well on paper towels and set aside. Save 3 tablespoons of the grease in the pan and discard the remainder.

Saute the onion for 5 minutes on medium-high heat in the bacon grease saved in the stock pot. Reduce the heat to medium, add the celery and cook for another 5 minutes.

Add stock and wild rice and bring to a boil. Reduce heat to medium-low, add the brown sugar and herbs and cook until the rice is split and soft, about 45-50 minutes.

Stir in the cream and heat through. If desired, for a thicker chowder type of soup, add a slurry of the cornstarch and cold water by whisking the cornstarch into the cold water and then add into the soup, a small amount at a time, until thickened to your taste. Add reserved bacon. Adjust seasonings.

Creamy Charred Poblano Soup

Janet Hickok
Servings 8

6	poblano peppers -- roasted and peeled
1	small onion -- diced
1	clove garlic -- minced
2	tablespoons olive oil
1/2	cup dry white wine
4	cups chicken broth -- or vegetable broth
1/2	teaspoon sugar
2	cups heavy cream
1	tablespoon cornstarch -- mixed with 2 tablespoons cold water to form a slurry
	Kosher or sea salt and fresh ground black pepper -- to taste

Place whole poblanos over a gas flame, or under the broiler. Turn repeatedly so that the entire chile is charred and blackened. Place in a paper or plastic bag and let steam for 20 minutes. Remove chilies from bag, peel off the skin, remove the stem, seeds and veins.

Meanwhile, saute onion and garlic in the olive oil over medium heat in a 4 quart stock pot. When the onion is translucent and starting to caramelize, deglaze the pot by adding the dry white wine. Add 3 cups of the chicken broth. While the stock simmers, place the chile peppers and the fourth cup of broth in a blender and puree until smooth. Add the stock/peppers mix to the pot and continue to simmer for 20 to 30 minutes.

Add sugar and cream, heat through. Whisk in cornstarch slurry. Stir until soup just comes to a boil, about 3-4 minutes. Reduce heat to medium-low and continue to cook for 5 minutes more. Remove from heat. Salt and pepper to taste.

Double Cheese Broccoli Soup

Janet Hickok
Servings 8

1	tablespoon olive oil
1/2	cup onions -- minced
1/4	cup celery -- minced
2	cups chicken broth
20	ounces frozen broccoli florets -- or frozen cuts
1	bay leaf
1	pinch oregano
1	pinch thyme
1	pound Velveeta Light ®-- cubed
1 1/2	cups shredded cheddar cheese
1	cup heavy cream -- or more if needed
1	pinch sugar
	Kosher or sea salt and fresh ground black pepper -- to taste

In a medium sized, heavy saucepan, on medium-high heat, saute onion and celery in olive oil until onion is translucent.

Add broth, broccoli and herbs; boil, covered, until broccoli is soft and on the verge of falling apart, approximately 30 minutes. Additional water may be needed so that the broccoli does not boil dry but there shouldn't be much liquid left at the end of this process.

Add cubed processed cheese, one cup of cheddar cheese and stir to melt and blend. Over medium heat, bring soup to just short of a boil. Reduce heat to low, add cream and sugar, stirring to blend. Adjust seasonings to taste.

Five Hour Stew

Vivian Hickok
Servings 18

4	pounds stew meat or wild game -- cubed
6	medium potatoes -- cubed
2	medium onions -- chopped
8	whole carrots -- peeled and chopped
1	20 ounce can whole tomatoes -- juice drained into a bowl
3	tablespoons tapioca -- instant
	Kosher or sea salt and fresh ground black pepper -- to taste
12	ounces V-8® vegetable juice
2	sprigs fresh thyme -- optional
2	bay leaves -- optional
1/2	teaspoon sage -- optional

Preheat oven to 300 degrees.

Combine raw meat and raw vegetables in a slow cooker or roasting pan with lid. Salt and pepper and add the herbs. Using a slotted spoon lift the tomatoes from the can and the juices and add to stew in the pan. Stir tapioca into the juice; let sit for 10-15 minutes; add this to the pan; mix well with meat and vegetables. This mix will appear dry and lumpy but the juices will seep out of the vegetables during cooking and will thicken with the tapioca. After 3 hours of cooking check the stew, stir and adjust the seasonings to your taste. Add the V-8® if needed. Cover and return to the oven for 2 more hours. Stir and check seasonings once more before serving.

This stew can be adjusted to your individual taste. I like mine thick, with extra tomatoes so I add more tapioca and tomatoes. Sometimes I add turnips, rutabagas and zucchini. Make the stew with your favorites; you'll find that just about anything will work (meat and vegetables) as this is a virtually fool-proof recipe!

Soups

Rustic Pasta and Bean Soup

Janet Hickok
Servings 6

12	slices bacon -- cut into 1/2 inch pieces
1	tablespoon olive oil
1	medium onion -- diced
1/2	cup celery -- diced
1	cup carrot -- cut into thin strips
2	cloves garlic -- minced
4	cups chicken stock
1 1/2	cups canned tomatoes -- drained and diced
1	can cannelini beans -- 16 ounce size
1	can garbanzo beans -- 16 ounce size
1 1/2	teaspoons sugar
1/2	teaspoon fresh ground black pepper
1/4	teaspoon fresh rosemary -- minced
2	tablespoons fresh parsley -- chopped
1/2	teaspoon oregano
2/3	cup pasta shells, cooked according to the package -- mini bow ties or similar size pasta

Saute the bacon pieces on medium-high heat in a large stockpot or dutch oven until well browned and crisp. Remove bacon, drain and set aside.

Discard all but 2 tablespoons of the grease. Use the olive oil and the reserved grease to saute the onion for 5 minutes. Add celery and carrots, saute another 5 minutes. Add garlic and cook, stirring, for 1 minute more.

Add stock, tomatoes, beans, sugar, flavorings and bring to a boil. Reduce heat to medium-low and simmer for 20 minutes.

Add the cooked pasta and simmer for 10-15 minutes more to blend flavors well. Adjust seasonings.

Shrimp and Corn Chowder

Janet Hickok
Servings 8

3	slices bacon -- chopped
2	onions -- medium, chopped
2	stalks celery -- chopped
4	carrots -- peeled, and cubed
1/3	cup flour
4	cups chicken stock
3	sprigs fresh thyme
1	teaspoon sugar
6	yellow flesh potatoes -- cubed
4	ounces chopped green chilis
5	cups frozen corn kernels -- thawed
1	cup whipping cream
2	pounds lump crabmeat -- or shrimp meat
1/2	cup chopped fresh parsley
	salt and pepper -- to taste

Saute bacon in a large saucepan over medium heat until fat is rendered and bacon is browned. Remove bacon pieces and add onion and celery to the fat and saute until translucent and soft; add carrot cubes and cook another 8 minutes. Sprinkle flour over vegetables and cook, stirring for five minutes. Stir in stock and whisk to combine until very smooth. Add thyme, sugar, potatoes, green chilis and corn and bring to a boil. Reduce to a simmer and cook until potatoes are soft and soup starts to thicken, stirring occasionally.

Stir cream into soup. When heated through but not boiling, add the seafood of your choice. If the seafood is raw it will take longer to cook through. Do not overcook the seafood. Remove thyme sprigs and add the reserved bacon, and fresh parsley. Season to taste with salt and pepper.

Fogged-In Split Pea Soup

Janet Hickok
Servings 8

2	tablespoons olive oil
1	medium onion -- diced, about 2/3 cup
2	stalks celery -- diced, about 2/3 cup
3	whole carrots -- peeled and sliced, or approximately 1 1/2 cups
6	cups chicken broth
2	cups split peas
2	sprigs fresh thyme
2	bay leaves
1/2	teaspoon sugar
1/4	teaspoon dried oregano -- or 2 sprigs of fresh Kosher or sea salt and freshly ground pepper -- to taste
1 1/2	cups extra lean ham -- diced

Saute onion and celery in olive oil on medium heat in a 6 or 8 quart stockpot. When onion is translucent, about 5 minutes, add carrots; saute 5-8 minutes longer. Add stock, herbs, and split peas to pot; bring to a boil. Reduce heat and simmer. When peas are starting to break down, about 30-40 minutes, add sugar, salt, and peppers. Remove bay leaves, thyme sprigs. Add ham bits and continue cooking until heated through. Adjust seasonings to your taste.

NOTE: I like my soups on the thick side, so if the soup seems a bit thin, I make a slurry of 1/4 cup cornstarch and 1/4 cup cold water and stir it into the bubbling soup, a bit at a time, until it thickens.

Cream of Potato Soup

Janet Hickok
Servings 8

1	tablespoon olive oil
1	medium onion -- diced
2	stalks celery -- diced
1	tablespoon butter
1	tablespoon all-purpose flour
1/2	cup carrot slices
2 1/2	cups chicken stock
1	bay leaf
5	medium red potatoes -- diced
2	cups heavy cream
1	teaspoon honey
	Kosher or sea salt and fresh ground black pepper -- to taste

Heat the olive oil in a large stock pot, add onion and celery. Cook until starting to soften and taking on a bit of color, about 12-15 minutes. Add the butter; allow to melt. Stir in flour and cook, stirring, for 2 minutes. Add carrots, chicken stock, and bay leaf. Bring to a boil.

Add potatoes and simmer for at least 30 minutes or until potatoes are cooked through, but not falling apart. Stir in honey and heavy cream and heat through. Remove bay leaf and adjust seasonings with salt and pepper.

If desired, for a richer looking, silky smooth soup, take 1/3 of the soup mixture and puree in a blender or food processor until thick and then add back into the pot.

Chicken and Rice Soup

Janet Hickok
Servings 8

1	cup diced onion
1	cup diced celery
3/4	cup diced carrots
2	cloves garlic -- minced
6	cups chicken broth
1 1/2	cups rice
4	cooked chicken breast halves -- chopped
2	tablespoons parsley -- chopped
1/2	teaspoon sugar
	salt and pepper -- to taste
1/2	cup peas -- optional
1	tablespoon cornstarch -- in 2 tablespoons cold water

Place 2 tablespoons olive oil in a large sized heavy saucepan on medium-high heat, saute onion and celery until onion is translucent. Add the carrot and garlic, saute for 3 minutes more. Do not allow garlic to brown. Add chicken broth to saucepan and bring to a boil. Add rice and sauteed chicken. When mixture returns to a boil, reduce heat to low and allow to simmer for at least 20 minutes or until rice is cooked through. Add parsley, sugar, salt and pepper to taste, and simmer another 10 minutes. Add peas, if using, at this time.

I like my soups a little on the thick side and often add a small amount of thickener to the broth. Equal amounts of cornstarch and cold water whisked together and stirred into the boiling broth works well. Start with 2 tablespoons of each and add a bit at a time until thickened to your liking. Boil for 3 minutes after adding to broth.

Uncannily Good Kraut Soup

Janet Hickok
Servings 12

1	tablespoon olive oil
1	pound bacon -- cut in 1" pieces, or your choice of sausage
1	large onion -- chopped fine
1/2	cup celery -- chopped fine
2	tablespoons tomato paste
1/4	teaspoon celery salt
2	teaspoons paprika
6	cups chicken stock -- or beef, if desired
2	medium baking potatoes -- cut in 1/4" cubes
2	cups sauerkraut -- rinsed and drained
2	cups heavy cream
1	teaspoon sugar
2	tablespoons fresh parsley -- chopped
	Kosher or sea salt and fresh ground black pepper -- to taste

Heat olive oil in a large, heavy stock pot, over medium-high heat. Add the bacon (or sausage) and cook, stirring often until bacon is crisp. Remove about two-thirds of the cooked bacon and drain on paper towels; set aside.

Discard all but 2 tablespoons of the bacon grease. Add onions and celery and cook for 10-15 minutes or until onions begin to soften. Add tomato paste, celery salt and paprika. Stir until well combined and the flavors are released. Add stock, potatoes and kraut; (I like to leave mine sour, but most might prefer the rinsed version) stir to blend. Once pot has come to a boil, reduce temperature to low and allow to simmer until the potatoes are soft, about 45-55 minutes. Stir in cream, sugar, parsley, and reserved bacon pieces. Simmer for another 15-20 minutes. Adjust seasonings with salt and pepper.

Roasted Tomato Soup

Janet Hickok
Servings 4

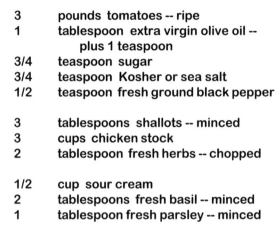

3	pounds tomatoes -- ripe
1	tablespoon extra virgin olive oil -- plus 1 teaspoon
3/4	teaspoon sugar
3/4	teaspoon Kosher or sea salt
1/2	teaspoon fresh ground black pepper
3	tablespoons shallots -- minced
3	cups chicken stock
2	tablespoon fresh herbs -- chopped
1/2	cup sour cream
2	tablespoons fresh basil -- minced
1	tablespoon fresh parsley -- minced
2	teaspoons lemon juice -- optional

Preheat the oven to 325 degrees. Cut the tomatoes in half lengthwise through the stem and quarter larger tomatoes. In a medium bowl, toss the tomatoes with the 1 tablespoon of olive oil to coat.

Arrange the tomatoes, cut side up, on a large foil lined baking sheet and sprinkle with salt, pepper and sugar. Roast the tomatoes for at least 2 hours, or until most of their juices have evaporated and they are just beginning to brown. The tomatoes should hold their shape when moved.

Heat the remaining 1 teaspoon of olive oil in a small skillet. Add the shallots, cover and cook until they are soft and beginning to brown, about 5 minutes. Transfer to a blender, add tomatoes and puree. With the machine running, drizzle in the chicken stock and process until incorporated. Pass the soup through strainer into a clean saucepan and bring to a simmer. Add the herbs of your choice, such as basil, thyme, fennel etc. and cook for another 10 minutes. Season to taste with salt and pepper.

Whisk together the sour cream, herbs and vinegar and drizzle on top of the warm soup.

Tortilla and Hominy Soup

Janet Hickok
Serves 15

6	corn tortillas, cut into strips
1	cup corn oil, for frying
3	medium onion, diced, divided
3	stalks celery, diced
2	teaspoons olive oil
6	chicken breasts, skinned, cut up
12	cups chicken stock
28	ounces canned tomatoes
4	cups yellow hominy
2	whole limes, juiced
1/2	cup cilantro, chopped
3	whole jalapeno chile peppers
1	teaspoon sugar
	Kosher salt and black pepper -- to taste
3	jalapeno chile peppers, diced fine
1	bunch cilantro, chopped
1	cup sour cream
3	limes, quartered

In a medium skillet, heat oil until shimmering. Test a strip of tortilla; when oil is hot enough, strips should turn golden in about 40 seconds. Fry in batches and drain on paper towels, set aside.

In a large stock pot saute 1 1/2 cups of the onion and the celery in olive oil until starting to soften. Add chicken breasts and saute until just done through and no longer pink. Set aside and keep warm. In the same pot, bring the stock to a boil and then reduce to a simmer. Add tomatoes, hominy, lime juice, jalapenos (whole with stems) and continue cooking for 15 minutes. Add the chicken and onion mix, simmer for another 10 minutes. Stir in sugar, salt, and pepper to taste.

Serve with fried tortilla strips, jalapenos, diced onion, cilantro, sour cream, and limes.

Hallo Bay Seafood Cioppino

Janet Hickok
Servings 8

4	pounds seafood -- mixed, your choice
3	cups white wine
1 1/2	cups water
2	tablespoons olive oil
1	large onion -- diced small
3	cups red and green bell peppers -- diced
2	cups canned tomatoes -- chopped
8	cups chicken stock
2	cups fish stock -- optional
2	teaspoons sugar
2	teaspoons curry paste -- or to taste
3	teaspoons Cioppino Seasoning, page 108
6	tablespoons butter
2	tablespoons lemon juice

Prepare seafood by cleaning and cutting into bite-sized and equal-sized pieces so that they will cook at the same rate. Set aside.

In a medium large stock pot, bring wine and water to a rapid, rolling boil; reduce by one third. Meanwhile, in a medium skillet over medium-high heat, saute the onions with the olive oil until softened and translucent. Add peppers and cook another 5 minutes. Add to stock pot. Add tomatoes, chicken stock, fish stock (or additional chicken stock), sugar, curry paste, and cioppino seasoning; lower heat to a simmer and cook for 30 minutes. Add seafood; turn off burner and let the heat of the stock cook the meat. Do not overcook the seafood. Stir in butter and lemon juice; serve immediately.

NOTE: I use shrimp, halibut, scallops, and salmon.

Savory White Bean and Bacon Soup

Janet Hickok
Serves 15

2	cups great northern beans, dried
1 1/2	tablespoons olive oil
1	large onion, diced
1	large tomato, diced
1 1/2	cups carrot slices
1/2	cup celery, chopped fine
4	cloves garlic, minced
6	slices bacon, thick-sliced, chopped
12	cups chicken stock
1 1/2	teaspoons fresh thyme
1	teaspoon fresh rosemary, minced fine
1	teaspoon fresh oregano, chopped fine
1	cup whipping cream, or half and half
	Kosher salt and fresh ground black pepper, to taste

Sort beans and remove any dark or discolored pieces. Soak in a large heavy stock pot overnight completely covered by 2 inches of cold water. After soaking, drain beans and set aside.

In the heavy stock pot, cook bacon pieces until crisp and fat is rendered. Remove bacon and drain on a paper towel and discard all but 2 tablespoons of the fat. Add olive oil to the bacon fat and turn to medium-high heat. Add onion and saute for 5 minutes. Add celery and carrots; saute another 5 minutes; stir occasionally. Add beans, tomatoes, herbs and 10 cups of stock and bring to a boil. Reduce heat to medium-low and let simmer until beans are very tender and soft, 1 - 1 1/2 hours.

Puree half of the soup in a processor or blender in batches. If some of the stock is needed at this time to thin the beans while blending, add in 1/4 cup increments. Return all to the pan, add cream and more stock if desired. Season to taste, add the reserved bacon and serve.

Salads

Spinach, Strawberry and Mandarin Salad with Sweet and Tangy Parsley Vinaigrette

Janet Hickok
Servings 20

2	each	celery ribs -- diced fine
1/2	teaspoon	celery salt
1	teaspoon	dry mustard
1	teaspoon	salt
1/3	cup	sugar
1/2	cup	parsley. chopped
1	cup	oil -- canola or vegetable
1/2	cup	cider vinegar
1	bag	spinach leaves -- stems removed
1	pint	strawberries -- sliced
12	ounces	mandarin oranges in light syrup -- drained

DRESSING: It is very quick and easy to use a food processor or blender to make this dressing. Pulse onions and celery until fine, add parsley and pulse. Add remaining dressing ingredients except oil and pulse until pureed. While machine is running, slowly pour in oil.

This makes about 2 cups. Use on salad to your taste. Dressing will keep in fridge for 2 weeks. Shake very well to combine before using.

Serve over lettuce and spinach leaves that have been tossed with the mandarin oranges, strawberries and Lisa's Sugared Almonds, page 55.

Lisa's Sugar Almonds

Lisa Bleak
Servings 24

6	**egg whites**
1 1/2	**cups sugar**
6	**cups slivered almonds**
1 1/2	**stick butter -- melted**

Preheat oven to 325 degrees.   Line a rimmed baking sheet with foil; set aside.

Beat egg whites at high speed until foamy. Gradually add sugar, beating until peaks form.

Fold in almonds. Pour melted butter into prepared pan and spread almond mixture over butter.

Bake for 15 minutes stir and bake another 15 minutes stir again. Thereafter, stir every 5-10 minutes until almonds are dry and toasty brown.

NOTE: These will appear like a failure, gummy and clumpy - be patient, they will turn out beautiful. Make extra and keep on hand for different salads and desserts etc. They are truly delicious and even make a great snack.

Catalina Fiesta Salad

Molly Hedgecock adapted by Janet Hickok
Servings 20

2	cans red kidney beans -- drained
2	each red and green pepper -- chopped
2	medium onion -- chopped
6	medium tomatoes -- chopped
2	cans black olives
2	bottles french dressing -- or Catalina Style
2	large bags corn chips -- or as needed
1	pound cheddar cheese -- grated

Mix together beans, peppers, onion and tomatoes. Pour dressing over and toss. Chill thoroughly. Just before serving add the cheese and chips.
If salad is not going to be eaten completely the chips can be served on the side. They will not last if dressed, but the remainder of the salad can be kept until the next day.

Catalina Style Dressing

Janet Hickok
Yield 2/3 cup

1/4	cup salad oil
1/4	cup ketchup
1	tablespoon sugar
1	tablespoon white wine vinegar
1	tablespoon lemon juice
1	teaspoon worcestershire sauce
1/2	teaspoon paprika
1/2	teaspoon salt
1/2	teaspoon pepper
1/4	teaspoon celery salt
1/4	teaspoon garlic powder

Combine all ingredients, whisking well. Store in covered container for up to 2 weeks.
Use with the Catalina Fiesta Salad.

Mustard Bacon Dressing with Spinach Salad

Janet Hickok
Servings 12

1/4	pound bacon -- reserve drippings
1 1/2	cup mayonnaise
1/2	small onion -- finely grated
1/4	cup vegetable oil
1/4	cup red wine vinegar
2	tablespoons sugar -- or to taste
1	tablespoon Dijon mustard
	Kosher or sea salt and pepper -- to taste
2	bunches fresh spinach -- stems removed, cleaned
4	eggs, hard-boiled -- peeled and chopped
12	cherry tomatoes -- halved

Cut bacon into one half inch pieces, cook on medium heat until browned and crispy. Drain bacon on paper towels and set aside, reserving 2-3 tablespoons of the grease.

Combine mayonnaise, onion, vegetable oil, vinegar, sugar and mustard in an electric blender or food processor. Whisk in reserved bacon drippings. Season with salt and pepper.

Place spinach in a large bowl or on 12 plates and top with the egg, tomatoes, and reserved bacon. Pass dressing on side.

This dressing is especially good on all types of spinach salads, but you will find it so delicious that you may want to try it on other salads or to top fresh cooked fish or chicken.

Garden Medley Pasta Toss

Janet Hickok
Servings 12

16	ounces marinated artichoke hearts -- drained and chopped, reserve marinade	
1/2	cup Italian salad dressing -- your favorite dry mix	
8	ounces pasta shells -- or rotini pasta	
1	tablespoon vegetable oil	
2	tablespoons cider vinegar	
2	teaspoons sugar	
1	clove garlic -- minced	
1	cup mayonnaise	
	salt and pepper -- to taste	
1	cup broccoli florets -- blanched, drained well	
1/2	cup frozen peas -- thawed	
10	cherry tomatoes -- halved	
1/2	cup black olives -- halved	

Drain and chop artichoke hearts, reserving the marinade. Whisk half of the reserved artichoke marinade and the dry Italian dressing mix until well blended and set aside.

Cook pasta in boiling, heavily salted water according to directions on package. Add tablespoon of oil to the water. Place broccoli florets in a metal mesh strainer or sieve. Plunge into the boiling water for 3 minutes. Remove; drain well. Continue with cooking the pasta. When pasta is al dente drain well. Place pasta in large bowl and cool.

In a small bowl whisk to combine marinade/dressing mix, vinegar, sugar, garlic and mayonnaise. Season with salt and pepper to taste. Fold into pasta until evenly distributed. Gently fold in chopped artichoke hearts, broccoli, peas, tomatoes and olives. Chill for several hours before serving.

Crunchy Noodle Slaw

Janet Hickok
Servings 12

1	medium head cabbage -- chopped or shredded (about 10 cups)
2	green onions -- chopped
2	3 ounce packages ramen -- noodles, uncooked
1/4	cup butter
1	tablespoon sesame seeds
1/2	cup slivered almonds
1/2	cup vegetable oil
1/4	teaspoon sesame oil
1	tablespoon soy sauce, low sodium
1/3	cup sugar
1/4	cup rice wine vinegar -- or cider vinegar

In a large bowl, combine cabbage and onions. Chill.

Meanwhile, break noodles into small pieces, throw out the seasoning packets. In a non-stick skillet, melt the butter over medium-low heat. Add noodles, sesame seeds and almonds. Cook until browned, stirring frequently. Drain on paper towel and keep at room temperature.

Combine vegetable and sesame oils, soy sauce, sugar, vinegar and whisk until well mixed. Twenty minutes before serving toss all ingredients together.

NOTE: I also like to make this a more complete meal by adding cooked chicken.
I keep extra cabbage, dressing and "crunchies" on hand so that I have a super quick lunch ready in seconds as this is one of my favorite salads.

Tooty-Frooty Black Bean and Bell Pepper Salad

Janet Hickok
Servings 8

1	large green bell pepper -- diced small
1	large red bell pepper -- diced small
1	jalapeno -- diced fine
1	small white onion -- diced small
1	mango -- peeled and chopped -- may use peaches, plums, or nectarines
4	cups black beans -- rinsed and drained
1/4	cup fresh cilantro -- chopped
1	tablespoon olive oil
1	tablespoon white vinegar
2	limes -- juiced
1	teaspoon cumin
2	teaspoons honey
	Kosher or sea salt and pepper -- to taste
	Romaine lettuce -- garnish
	Cilantro sprigs -- garnish

Combine peppers, jalapeno, onion, fruit, beans and cilantro in a large bowl.

Whisk together oil, vinegar, lime juice, cumin, honey, salt, and pepper. Pour over salad ingredients and fold together.

Let chill for at least 2-3 hours for flavors to blends. Line serving bowl with lettuce leaves and garnish with cilantro.

Jim K's Cherry-Cola Gelatin

Servings 18

1 1/2	**cups water**
6	**ounces cherry gelatin powder -- or berry flavor of choice**
1	**can cherry pie filling**
1	**can diet cola -- 12 ounce size, or regular if desired**

Boil water and whisk in dry gelatin until dissolved. Remove from heat Carefully pour in cola. Skim off foam. Place pie filling into serving bowl(s); pour gelatin over; stir to combine. Chill until set.

NOTE: Make sure that your gelatin is completely dissolved before adding to the pie filling.
Stir gelatin very gently one time, 15 minutes after placing in fridge to chill and set, so that the cherries are evenly distributed.

Seafoam Salad

Janet Hickok
Servings 18

1	**6 ounce gelatin -- lime flavored**
2	**cans pears -- 16 ounces each**
8	**ounces cream cheese -- softened**
1 1/2	**cups whipped topping**

Pour juice off of pears into a small saucepan and bring liquid to a boil. Add gelatin, whisking to blend completely. Set aside.

Meanwhile combine cream cheese and pear halves in a food processor and pulse to mix to a very smooth consistency. Scrape down sides as needed. Carefully add gelatin, pulsing once or twice to incorporate. Pour into mixing bowl and fold in whipped topping.

Pour into serving bowls and chill until set.
Garnish with lime slices and or edible flowers if desired.

Wall Street Salad and Dressing

James Wright
Servings 20

1	package Italian salad dressing -- dry mix
1/2	large lemon -- juiced
1	tablespoon sugar
1/2	purple onion -- sliced paper-thin
1	pint cherry tomatoes -- halved
3/4	cup blue cheese -- crumbled
1	head green leaf lettuce -- torn
1	head romaine lettuce -- torn

Mix your favorite Italian dressing mix according to package directions. Add lemon juice and sugar and shake to mix well until sugar is completely dissolved.

Tear lettuce into pieces, toss in tomatoes, place in large bowl. Place onion rings on top. Sprinkle with cheese. Pour dressing over and serve immediately.

Southern Style Slaw Dressing

Molly Hedgecock adapted by Janet Hickok
Yield 1 3/4 cup

1	cup mayonnaise
1	tablespoon fresh lemon juice
1/2	cup sugar
1/4	cup vinegar
1/8	teaspoon celery salt
1/4	teaspoon Kosher or sea salt -- to taste
1/8	teaspoon pepper -- to taste
1	medium head of cabbage -- shredded

Whisk together all ingredients and pour over shredded cabbage and let set for at least one hour or up to 4 hours before serving. This will cover one medium to large head of cabbage.
I find it easier to make plenty of dressing and discard or save unused portion.

Try It, You'll Like It Salad

Servings 8

1	head broccoli -- cut into bite-sized pieces
1/2	red onion -- diced fine
1	cup raisins
1	cup sunflower seeds
6	slices bacon -- chopped and fried crisp
1	cup mayonnaise
1/4	cup sugar
2	tablespoons red wine vinegar

Place broccoli, onion, and raisins in a medium bowl. Whisk mayonnaise, sugar and vinegar together and pour over ingredients. This step can be done up to 6 hours ahead of time. Chill.

No more than one hour before serving, fold in the sunflower seeds and bacon until well combined. Chill until ready to serve.

Barrett Salad

Susan Barrett
Servings 8

1	head romaine lettuce -- torn into pieces
1	package Italian salad dressing -- or your choice of bottled
1/4	cup sesame seeds -- toasted
1/2	cup Romano cheese -- grated
1/2	avocado -- cubed

Use your favorite Italian dressing. Toss lettuce with desired amount of dressing. Mix well. Toss in remaining ingredients. Serve immediately.

This salad is delicious and so easy. It tastes much better than its simplicity, and list of ingredients, predicts.

Seven-Up Salad

Mildred Bridges
Servings 18

6	ounces lemon gelatin powder
2	cups hot water
2	cups lemon-lime soda
1	cup marshmallows -- miniature
2	large bananas
14	ounces canned pineapple chunks -- drained, juice reserved
1 1/4	cups frozen blueberries -- optional
1	cup pineapple juice -- from reserved
1/2	cup sugar
2	tablespoons flour
1	egg -- slightly beaten
2	tablespoons butter
1/2	pint whipped topping
1/2	cup grated cheddar cheese -- optional

Dissolve jello in hot water; stir in soda, marshmallows and fruit. Chill. If using blueberries, distribute evenly over top of gelatin after it has chilled for 20 minutes and while preparing the topping.

In a small heavy saucepan bring 1 cup reserved juice, sugar, flour, egg, and butter to a slow boil, whisking constantly until thick. Cool completely and whisk into whipped topping. Pour over set jello and sprinkle with cheese. Chill until serving.

Black Eyed Bob Salad

Bob Caton
Servings 6

3	tablespoons	red wine vinegar
2	tablespoons	vegetable oil
2	tablespoons	hot sauce
2	tablespoons	fresh cilantro -- chopped
1	clove	garlic -- minced
1/2	teaspoon	Kosher or sea salt
31	ounces	black-eyed peas -- rinsed, drained
1	medium	purple onion -- diced fine
1	medium	tomato -- seeded and diced
1	medium	green bell pepper -- diced
		green leaf lettuce -- for garnish

Whisk first 6 ingredients in a large bowl; add black eyed peas and next 3 ingredients, tossing to coat. Cover and chill at least 2 hours. Serve on lettuce-lined platter.

Marvelous Marinated Cukes

Janet Hickok
Servings 12

3	large	cucumbers -- peeled and sliced
1	cup	vinegar -- cider preferably
2	tablespoons	cider or rice wine vinegar
1	teaspoon	Kosher or sea salt
1/2	teaspoon	black pepper
2	tablespoons	sugar
1/2	tablespoon	red pepper flakes -- or to taste
2	tablespoons	olive oil

Thickly slice the cucumbers; place in a gallon size, zip top plastic bag. Whisk all other ingredients until sugar is dissolved and place along with the cucumbers in plastic bag; remove all air so that marination is even. Chill.
Allow to sit at room temperature for 1 hour before serving.

King Midas' Gold Potato Salad

Janet Hickok
Servings 8

3	pounds potatoes -- peeled, cut into 1 inch pieces
4	eggs -- hardboiled, peeled
6	sweet pickles -- chopped fine
6	dill pickles -- chopped fine
1	cup celery -- diced
1	cup onions -- diced
1	teaspoon dry mustard
1/2	cup prepared mustard
2	tablespoons dill pickle juice
1	cup light mayonnaise
1/4	cup sour cream
1	tablespoon sugar

Boil potatoes in very salty water until just tender. Chop eggs. In a small bowl, combine mayonnaise, milk, onion, celery, sweet pickle, dill pickles and pickle juice, mustards, and remainder of ingredients. Salt and pepper to taste. Adjust seasonings, fold in potatoes and egg. Let chill for 2 hours.

Melon Fresh

Janet Hickok
Servings 8

2	cantaloupes -- cut in 1" pieces
1/2	cup sour cream
2	teaspoons powdered sugar
1	pinch nutmeg
2	teaspoons fresh mint -- minced, Optional

Combine dressing ingredients and use a whisk to create a creamy smooth appearance. Add mint if desired. Toss gently with the melon pieces just before serving, and use only enough to just coat.
NOTE: Mix this together just before serving.

Lemony Shrimp and Orzo Salad

Janet Hickok
Servings 4

1 1/2	cups cold water
1	pound medium-size shrimp -- peeled, deveined
1	cup uncooked Orzo
1 1/2	cups plum tomatoes -- diced
1/4	cup green onions -- thinly sliced
1/2	cup fresh basil -- chopped
1/2	cup canned low sodium chicken broth
3	tablespoons fresh lemon juice
1	tablespoon olive oil
1	teaspoon sugar
1/4	teaspoon salt
1/4	teaspoon pepper
1/2	cup fresh grated Parmesan cheese

Bring water to a boil in a medium saucepan. Add shrimp; cook 3 minutes. Drain shrimp in a colander over a bowl, reserving liquid. Add orzo to reserved liquid. Cover and bring back to a boil for 5 minutes. Let stand 5 minutes; drain. Fluff with a fork. Combine orzo, shrimp, tomatoes, green onions, and basil in a large bowl. Combine broth, lemon juice, oil, sugar, salt and pepper. Pour dressing over salad; toss gently to coat. Sprinkle with cheese.

Balsamic Vinaigrette

Janet Hickok
Makes 1 2/3 cup

1/2	cup balsamic vinegar
3	tablespoons dijon mustard
3	tablespoons honey
2	clove garlic, minced
2	small shallot, minced
1/4	teaspoon Kosher salt
1/4	teaspoon black pepper
3/4	cup olive oil

Whisk together first 7 ingredients until blended. Gradually whisk in olive oil.

Grilled Fruit, Gorgonzola and Toasted Walnut Salad

Janet Hickok
Serves 8

12	cups lettuce leaves, mixed variety, washed and dried
4	pears, nectarines, apples, or plums
1	cup gorgonzola cheese, crumbled
1	1/2 cups walnuts, toasted

Cut fruit in half and core or pit. Heat grill to high, or heat a heavy skillet over medium-high heat. Melt butter and brush cut side of fruit. Place cut side down on grill and cook until marked by grill and softened, 10-15 minutes. Carefully remove from grill and allow to cool.

Divide mix of lettuce leaves such as red and green leaf, butter, radicchio, romaine, and/or red oak on 8 plates. Arrange a piece of fruit on side of plate, top with gorgonzola cheese, walnuts and drizzle with Balsamic Vinaigrette, page 67.

NOTE: I have tried pear, nectarine and plum with this salad and all are extremely delicious.

Raspberry, Strawberry or Blueberry Vinegar

Janet Hickok
Makes Approximately 5 cups

4	cups frozen strawberries, blueberries or raspberries
3 1/2	cups white wine vinegar, to cover

Place berries in a gallon glass jar or other glass container. Do Not Use Metal. Cover with white wine vinegar and let set for 2-3 days at room temperature, covering with cheese cloth only. Strain well through another piece of cheesecloth or a fine stainer.

Now you have fresh berry vinegar for dressings.

71

72

Vegetables

Seared Balsamic-Ginger Glazed Oriental Long Beans

Janet Hickok
Servings 4

1	tablespoon balsamic vinegar -- plus 2 teaspoons
1	teaspoon brown sugar
2	tablespoons olive oil
10	ounces green beans -- trimmed
2	cloves garlic -- minced
2	teaspoons fresh grated ginger
1	teaspoon minced shallot
	Kosher or sea salt and fresh ground black pepper -- to taste
1/4	cup water -- or more if needed
1	tablespoon unsalted butter -- cut into pieces
1	tablespoon sliced almonds -- toasted

Whisk one tablespoon of the balsamic vinegar with the sugar in a small bowl; set aside.

Heat a heavy skillet or large wok over high heat for 2 minutes. Pour in the oil and heat until shimmering, 20-30 seconds. Add the green beans, garlic, ginger, and shallot. Season with salt and pepper and cook, stirring often, until they brown and shrivel, 3-4 minutes.

Reduce the heat to medium low, carefully add the water and the vinegar/brown sugar mixture. Stir the beans; cover the pan with the lid ajar. Cook until the beans are tender but still have a slight crunch, about 4 minutes more. Stir in the remaining balsamic vinegar.

Add the butter and almonds and toss until the butter is melted. Adjust seasonings.

If you can get them, the green, Oriental long bean add an extra gourmet touch. Regular fresh green beans work just as well.

Chow-Chow Sper-Relish

Duane and Rayetta Sperl
Servings 48

1	head cabbage -- small
2	cups tomatoes -- green, chopped
2	cups green bell peppers -- chopped
3	cups cauliflower -- chopped
2	cups onions -- chopped
3	tablespoons salt
1 1/2	cups sugar
2	teaspoons celery seed
2	teaspoons dry mustard
1	teaspoon mustard seed
1	teaspoon turmeric
2 1/2	cups vinegar
1/2	teaspoon ground ginger

Combine first 5 ingredients (chopped vegetables) and sprinkle with the salt. Let stand 4-6 hours in a cool place.

Combine the next seven ingredients and simmer for 10 minutes. Add the vegetables and simmer another 10 minutes, then bring to a rolling boil.
Pour boiling hot into 4-6 pint jars leaving 1/4 inch headspace.
Adjust caps and process 10 minutes in a boiling water bath.

Looney's Cashew and Honey Vegetables

Carol Lynn Looney
Servings 8

1/2	stick butter
1	cup cashews -- chopped
1/4	cup honey
	Salt and pepper to taste
4	cups vegetables -- fresh blanched green beans or zucchini and yellow squash

Bring butter to a bubble and let brown lightly, add cashews and stir until slightly browned. Add honey and allow to boil for 1 minute. Stir into assorted vegetables of choice.

Mushroon Saute

Alan Latimer
Servings 6

2	tablespoons olive oil
1	tablespoon butter
1 1/2	pounds mushrooms -- cleaned, sliced
1/2	white onion -- diced
2	ounces garlic -- chopped
1	tablespoon fresh basil -- chopped
	black pepper -- to taste
	white wine -- Optional

Heat oil and butter in skillet. Add mushrooms and onions, saute for 6 minutes. Add garlic and basil, saute 4 minutes. Add cracked pepper and wine to taste. Saute 2 minutes.

Red Chile-Green Onion Butter for Corn on the Cob

Tracey Drummond
Yield 1 1/2 cups

2	sticks unsalted butter
2	tablespoons chili powder -- preferably ancho
2	cloves garlic -- minced
1/4	cup chopped green onions
2	tablespoons fresh lime juice
	Kosher salt and fresh pepper -- to taste

In a food processor, combine the butter, ancho chili powder, garlic, green onions, and lime juice and season with salt and pepper. Process until completely mixed.

Place a sheet of parchment or waxed paper on a work surface. Form the butter into a roll about 1 inch in diameter and place along the long side of the paper, leaving a border of 1 inch. Roll up the butter in the paper and chill for 30 minutes. The butter may also be frozen.

When ready to serve, brush generously on grilled corn on the cob, or pass with hot corn.

Swede's Zucchini Cakes

Swede Altaffer
Servings 8

2	cups zucchini -- shredded
1/2	cup cheddar cheese -- grated
1/2	cup grated onions -- or to taste
1/2	cup Bisquick® baking mix
2	eggs
1	jalapeno -- minced, or to taste

Combine all ingredients. Fry in batches in a nonstick skillet over medium-high heat in small amount of butter and/or oil, until golden brown, about 3-4 minutes on each side.

Satiny Garlic Cream Flan

Janet Hickok
Servings 16

1	tablespoon	roast garlic puree
6	large	eggs
1/8	teaspoon	brown sugar
1	teaspoon	Kosher or sea salt
1/4	teaspoon	white pepper
2	cups	heavy whipping cream

Preheat the oven to 325 degrees. Butter 16, 8 ounce ramekins or one large or two medium tart pans.

In a bowl whisk the garlic puree with the eggs, sugar, salt and pepper. Set aside.

In medium saucepan on medium-high heat, bring the cream just to the boiling point, or heat in a glass measuring cup in the microwave until just boiling, about 4 minutes. Carefully temper the hot cream into the egg mixture, by pouring in a steady even stream and whisking constantly. When all is well blended, carefully pour equal amounts into the ramekins and place them in a hot water bath.
Bake for 30-40 minutes. Transfer to a rack and let stand for 10 minutes. Serve from the ramekins or turn them out onto plates before serving.

This dish is especially delicious if the flans are topped with selection of roasted or grilled, chopped vegetables. I use onion, tomato, zucchini, mushrooms, and red and yellow bell peppers.

Heartland Corn Pudding

Janet Hickok

Servings 8

2	tablespoons butter
1/4	cup onion -- minced
3	cups frozen corn kernels -- thawed
2	cups heavy cream
6	large eggs
2	tablespoons all-purpose flour
1 1/2	teaspoons Kosher or sea salt
1 1/2	teaspoons sugar
1/4	teaspoon white pepper
1/4	cup fresh basil -- julienned
1/2	cup parmesan cheese -- grated, optional

Preheat oven to 350 degrees. Lightly butter a 2 quart baking dish.

Melt butter in a skillet over medium heat. Add onions and saute for 2-3 minutes. Set aside.

In a large bowl, whisk together the cream, eggs, flour, salt, sugar and white pepper. When smooth, fold in the corn, onion, and basil. Pour into prepared dish. (Can be prepared up to 8 hours ahead, cover and chill.)

Bake in a hot water bath until custard is set in center and knife inserted into center comes out clean, about 50 minutes. If topping with parmesan cheese, add to corn pudding about 20 minutes before finished baking, or remove when softened and melted.

Street Vendor Style Corn

Janet Hickok
Servings 10

2	pounds frozen corn kernels
1 1/2	teaspoons brown sugar
1/4	cup butter -- at room temperature
1/4	cup sour cream
1/4	cup mayonnaise
1/4	teaspoon cayenne pepper -- or to taste
1/2	cup chopped green chiles
1/4	cup parmesan cheese -- shredded
1/4	cup feta cheese -- crumbled
1/3	cup chopped cilantro
1	whole lime -- juiced

In a large skillet on high heat, cook corn and brown sugar until starting to brown, using a small amount of butter. Once corn is heated through and has a bit of color, remove from heat; stir in the butter, sour cream, mayo, cayenne pepper, chiles, and cheeses. Return to stove and heat very gently to warm through. Stir in lime, cilantro and salt and pepper to taste.

Tres Corn Casserole

Carol LiaBraaten
Servings 16

16	ounces frozen yellow corn
16	ounces each white and yellow hominy, canned -- drained
7	ounces green chiles -- diced, canned
1	cup sour cream -- or more if needed
1	pound cheddar cheese, shredded -- or Monterrey Jack

Preheat oven to 325 degrees. Grease a 2 quart baking dish, set aside.
Reserve 1/2 to 1 cup of the cheese. Stir remainder of ingredients together until evenly mixed. Sprinkle reserved cheese on top. Bake for 40 minutes without a lid. Serve piping hot.

Cumin-Braised Brussels Sprouts

Janet Hickok
Servings 12

2 1/2	pounds Brussels sprouts
1	tablespoon butter
1	teaspoon olive oil
1	teaspoon whole cumin seeds

| 2 | tablespoons butter |
| | Kosher or sea salt and freshly ground black pepper -- to taste |

Trim and discard stem ends from Brussels sprouts; rinse sprouts. Cut each in half through stem end.

Add butter, olive oil, cumin seeds and Brussels sprouts to a 6 quart pan over high heat; stir often until sprouts are slightly browned, about 5 mintues. Add 1 cup water; cover, reduce heat to medium-high heat, and cook, stirring occasionally, until sprouts are tender when pierced, 6 to 8 minutes. If liquid evaporates before sprouts are done, add small amount water to keep from scorching.

Uncover and add butter; stir often until butter is melted. Salt and pepper to taste.

Bell Pepper and Summer Squash Saute

Janet Hickok
Servings 12

1/2	cup	olive oil
1/4	cup	corn oil
6	tablespoons	red wine vinegar
2	teaspoons	honey
3	cloves	garlic -- minced
6	teaspoons	fresh thyme -- or 1 1/2 teaspoons dry
1	tablespoon	fresh basil -- chopped
1 1/2	teaspoons	Kosher salt
3/4	teaspoon	fresh ground black pepper
2	large	red bell peppers -- chopped
2	large	yellow bell peppers -- chopped
1	large	green bell pepper -- chopped
2	medium	zucchini -- chopped
2	cups	button mushrooms -- halved

Mix all ingredients. Whisk well and pour over chopped vegetables and let sit for at least 1 hour. Stir fry over high heat until tender crisp.

Side Dishes

Herb & Parmesan Grilled Reds

Janet Hickok
Servings 8

3	pounds small red potatoes -- cleaned
4	tablespoons olive oil, divided
1/2	stick butter
3	tablespoons fresh parsley -- minced,
1	teaspoon dried basil
1/2	teaspoon garlic powder
1	teaspoon seasoned salt
1 1/2	teaspoons brown sugar
3	tablespoons freshly grated parmesan cheese

In large pot of boiling, salted water, cook potatoes for 15 minutes, or until a knife will pierce them. Drain potatoes and cool. Preheat grill. Cut potatoes in half vertically and transfer to large bowl. Add 2 tablespoons oil and toss to coat. Grill potatoes until golden, turning occasionally, about 15 minutes. Transfer to a large bowl and drizzle with remaining oil and remainder of ingredients. Toss gently to thoroughly coat. Adjust seasonings to taste.

Whitcomb's Potato Wedges

Mike Whitcomb
Servings 6

4	medium baking potatoes
1/4	cup olive oil
1/2	teaspoon Kosher or sea salt
1/4	teaspoon fresh ground black pepper
1/2	teaspoon basil leaves -- thyme and/or oregano
1/4	teaspoon paprika
1/2	cup dry parmesan

Preheat oven to 450 degrees. Line a rimmed baking sheet or 9x13 pan with foil. Cut potatoes lengthwise into wedges. Combine oil and seasonings and toss well with potatoes. Spread on pan and bake for 15 minutes. Stir. Turn oven to 350 degrees, and bake for 30 minutes. Remove from oven stir, sprinkle with the parmesan cheese. Bake for an additional 15 minutes.

Baked Beans Picnic Style

Janet Hickok
Servings 18

6	cups beans -- dried
1	cup vinegar
1	cup molasses
1	onion -- diced
1	16 ounce can tomato sauce
1	16 ounce can stewed tomatoes
1	cup prepared mustard
2	teaspoons garlic -- minced
	Salt -- and pepper to taste

Pre-soak beans overnight (or wash and bring to a boil in enough water to cover by 3" and boil for 45 minutes).
Drain. Add new water, enough to just cover the beans, and cook on medium heat until beans are tender but not mushy. Add water as needed to keep beans moist while cooking. When soft enough to bite through, drain all but I inch of the water off and add the remaining ingredients. Simmer on low for 1 hour, stirring occasionally. Place in baking dish and cook uncovered for 1 1/2 hours until meltingly tender.

Caramelized Yellow Onions

Janet Hickok
Servings 8

12	large sweet onions
3	teaspoons brown sugar
4	tablespoons butter
	Kosher salt and fresh ground black pepper

Peel onions and cut into 1/2 inch wide crescents.
Melt butter in a large nonstick skillet or cast iron fry pan. Add sugar and stir to dissolve. Add onions and cook over medium-high heat until starting to brown. Stir only occasionally so that onions have time to cook and caramelize throughout. Salt and pepper to taste. If necessary, cook in two batches as the onions brown better when the pan is not crowded. Serve with grilled steaks.

Natalia's Arroz Con Pollo

Natalia from Laredo
Servings 4

1	whole chicken -- cut into pieces
	olive oil -- for browning
1	cup rice
2	cups chicken broth
1	teaspoon peppercorns
1	teaspoon cumin seeds
2	cloves garlic -- medium size
4	ounces tomato sauce
	Salt -- to taste
2	serrano or jalapeno chiles -- whole, do not cut

In a casuela (a Mexican pottery casserole dish) or a dutch oven, pour a small amount of olive oil to brown the chicken pieces. When all pieces are completely browned, remove and keep warm. Another small amount of olive oil is needed to brown the rice, stirring occasionally. Meanwhile place peppercorns, garlic, and cumin seeds in a molcajete (mortar) and grind until fine. When rice is browned add chicken stock, chiles, seasonings and tomato sauce; stir to combine and then place the chicken evenly spaced around the casuela. Cover and cook over low heat for 20 minutes or until all liquid is absorbed and rice is cooked.

Spiced Sweet Potato Bake with Pecans

Janet Hickok
Servings 12

4	cups brown sugar, packed
14	ounces cinnamon candies
4	tablespoons cinnamon
1/2	teaspoon ground clove
1/2	teaspoon mace
1/2	teaspoon cardamom
2	teaspoons ground ginger
1/2	teaspoon ground nutmeg
4	pounds sweet potatoes -- or as needed
2	teaspoons Kosher or sea salt -- or to taste
3	cups miniature marshmallows -- or to taste
1 1/2	cups pecans

Combine all the spice ingredients and seal in a ziploc bag. This amount will make enough for more than one time. I make extra and keep it on hand.

Bake or steam your sweet potatoes until very soft. I like to cut in half lengthwise and place cut side down in a baking dish. Add a small amount of water to create steam and then cover well with foil and bake at 375 degrees, until knife inserts easily into potato flesh, about 45-55 minutes. Let cool for just a minute or two and then remove skins and place in a deep bowl or in an electric mixing bowl. Whisk to remove all lumps; add salt to taste. Add as little or as much of the spice mixture as you like and then turn into a greased baking dish. Bake until heated through. Remove from oven and top with a few marshmallows and a sprinkling of pecans and return to the oven to bake until marshmallows are golden.

Wild Mushroom and Roast Garlic Risotto

Janet Hickok
Servings 6

3/4	pound sliced fresh mushrooms -- your choice
6	cloves garlic -- roasted
3	tablespoons olive oil
1/4	cup finely chopped yellow onion
2	tablespoons fresh thyme -- chopped,
1 1/2	cups arborio rice
1/2	cup dry white wine
3 1/2	cups vegetable broth -- or more if needed (you may substitute chicken broth)
1/4	cup butter
1/4	cup heavy cream -- or as needed
1/3	cup grated fresh Parmesan cheese

Heat 1 tablespoon olive oil in a large nonstick skillet over medium-high heat. Add fresh mushrooms and saute until golden and juices evaporate, about 7 minutes. Season with salt and pepper. Set aside.

Heat 2 tablespoons olive oil in heavy, medium sized saucepan over medium-high heat. Add onion and thyme; saute until tender, about 4 minutes. Add arborio rice and stir to coat with onion mix. Add wine and cook until almost evaporated, stirring frequently. Mix in garlic and 1/2 cup of your choice of broth and bring to a boil. Reduce heat to medium and cook, stirring frequently, until rice is tender and mix is creamy. Add remainder of broth, by 1/2 cup measures as it evaporates and is absorbed by the risotto, about 20-30 minutes. Add mushroom mix. Stir in cream, butter, and cheese until melted and evenly distributed. Season to taste with salt and pepper.

Mexican Pinto Beans Authentico

Janet Hickok
Servings 10

1	pound pinto beans
1	medium onion -- diced
2	cloves garlic -- crushed
1	medium tomato -- diced
1/2	medium green bell pepper -- diced
1	pinch sugar
3	tablespoons fresh cilantro -- chopped
2	whole jalapeno chile peppers
1	teaspoon Kosher or sea salt -- or to taste

Sort the beans. Soak overnight or for 8-10 hours, in enough water to cover by 3-4 inches. Drain and rinse.

Place beans in a large stock pot and fill with enough water to cover beans by 2 inches. Bring to a boil.

Reduce heat to medium-low and cook for 30 minutes. Add onion, garlic, tomato, bell pepper, sugar, cilantro, and whole jalapenos (do not remove stems). Continue to cook until beans are soft to the bite, but still hold their shape, about 2 hours more. Stir occasionally and check water level. You will want the liquid to be just level with the beans. Season to taste with salt during the last hour of cooking - if added too early, the beans will not soften.

These beans are great the following day as refried beans. Just place in a skillet over medium-high heat and cook through, mashing coarsely with a fork. The authentic way is to add a large portion of lard at this point, but they are nearly as good with a small amount of bacon or sausage added to boost the flavor.

Orzo, Broccoli, Feta and Olive Quartet

Servings 24

6	cups orzo -- 24-28 ounce size
1	bunch broccoli -- cut into florets
1	cup olive oil -- or as needed
3/4	cup pine nuts
2	teaspoons red pepper flakes
3	cups feta cheese -- crumbled, about 14 ounces
32	ounces black olives -- halved
2	cups parmesan cheese -- grated
1	cup basil -- chopped

Cook orzo in a pot of boiling water until tender but still firm to bite, about 8 minutes. Without draining the pasta water, add broccoli and cook until crisp tender, about 4 minutes more.

Meanwhile, heat olive oil in a heavy sauce pan over medium heat. Add pine nuts and stir until golden brown, about 3 minutes. Add red pepper flakes and stir until aromatic, about 30 seconds. Remove from heat.

Drain orzo and broccoli. Transfer to a large bowl.

Pour oil/pine nut mix over pasta and toss to coat. Add feta, olives, parmesan and basil. Toss to mix. Season with salt and pepper to taste.

NOTE: This recipe is delicious as a side dish or as an entree if you'd like. Add shrimp or chicken to make it a very filling main dish. It is also great the second day as a cold or room temperature salad.

Pan-Fried Sweet Onion Baby Cakes

Joyce and Erica Jossi
Servings 10

1 1/4	cups all-purpose flour
2	tablespoons baking powder
1	tablespoon sugar
1/2	teaspoon salt
1	tablespoon cornmeal
6	ounces flattened beer
2 1/2	cups sweet onions -- diced fine
1	tablespoon Kosher salt
1	tablespoon sugar
1/2	cup vegetable oil

Combine the first five, dry ingredients; set aside,
Place the diced onion in a medium sized bowl and toss with the sugar and salt; pour into a sieve and let drain for 1 hour.

Fold the onion and dry ingredient mix together. Add just enough of the flat beer to make a thick batter.

Using approximately 3 tablespoons, portion out the cakes and fry in a small amount of hot oil in a non-stick skillet, until golden. Turn; fry on the other side until golden. Remove and drain on paper towel and keep warm until finished with all cakes. Serve immediately.

Hazelnut Wild Rice Pilaf

Janet Hickok
Servings 8

2	cups	wild rice
5 1/2	cups	chicken stock

1/2	cup	celery -- diced small
2	tablespoons	olive oil

1	cup	hazelnuts -- toasted, chopped
2	cups	fresh mushrooms, chopped
1/4	cup	chopped fresh thyme -- or to taste
4	each	green onions -- sliced
		Kosher or sea salt and fresh ground black pepper -- to taste
2	tablespoons	orange rind -- grated
1/3	cup	fresh squeezed orange juice

Simmer rice and stock for 45 minutes or until tender, but not over cooked.

Meanwhile, saute celery in 2 tablespoons olive oil until soft, about 10 minutes.

Drain rice, add remaining ingredients and stir to combine. Can be made ahead and re-heated in the microwave or kept hot in oven on low.

Sage, Sausage and Bread Dressing

Janet Hickok
Servings 12

1	pound sausage, optional
1	cup chopped celery
1	medium onion -- diced
1/2	cup butter
2	cups sliced fresh mushrooms
2 1/2	teaspoons chopped fresh sage
1/4	cup chopped fresh parsley
1/4	teaspoon each Kosher salt and black pepper
8	cups bread cubes
3/4	cup chicken broth

Fry sausage in a large skillet until browned and crumbly. Remove sausage and drain. In same skillet, saute celery and onion for 10 minutes. Add butter and mushrooms and cook for 10 minutes more. Stir in herbs.

Place bread cubes in a large bowl and stir in onion/celery mixture. Season with salt and pepper to taste. Carefully fold in broth. Adjust seasonings.

Bake in a well greased, 4 quart casserole, covered, in a 325 degree oven for 40 minutes. Remove cover and bake another 12 minutes or until top has browned and crisped.

Rustic Garlicky Tomato-Asparagus Tart

Janet Hickok
Servings 12

1	**whole puff pastry sheet**
3	**large eggs**
1	**teaspoon olive oil**
4	**cloves garlic, minced**
1/2	**teaspoon sugar**
1/8	**teaspoon Kosher or sea salt**
1	**tablespoon tomato paste**
1	**teaspoon fresh oregano, chopped, or thyme**
1	**tablespoon fresh basil, chopped**
1/8	**teaspoon fresh ground black pepper**
2	**cups canned tomatoes, seeded, peeled, and chopped**
1/3	**cup heavy cream**
2	**large tomatoes, sliced 1/4-inch thick**
1	**ounce Swiss cheese, shredded**
12	**stalks asparagus -- trimmed**
1	**ounce grated fresh Parmesan cheese, optional**

Preheat oven to 400 degrees.

Whisk eggs lightly. Trim pastry sheet by 1/2 inch all around and then using a small bit of the whisked egg, brush edges of remaining pastry and press cut strips on edges to create a rim. Place on a foil-lined baking sheet coated with cooking spray. Set aside.

Meanwhile, in a small skillet saute the garlic in the olive oil on medium-high for 1 minute. Then, to the remainder of the beaten eggs, add the garlic, sugar, salt, tomato paste, herbs, and pepper. Whisk until smooth. Whisk in cream until smooth. Stir in the chopped tomatoes and Swiss cheese. Pour into prepared crust. Top with sliced tomatoes and asparagus; sprinkle on the parmesan cheese.

Bake until set, and knife inserted in center comes out clean, about 40-45 minutes. Remove from oven and let set for 15-20 minutes before slicing.

Sauces and Seasonings

Onion, Dill and Pickle Tartar Sauce

Janet Hickok
Servings 40

2	cups	diced onions
1 1/2	cups	dill pickles -- chopped
1 1/2	tablespoons	worcestershire sauce
1/8	cup	fresh lemon juice
1	teaspoon	horseradish -- or to taste
1/2	tablespoon	sugar
1/2	teaspoon	garlic -- minced fine
1	tablespoon	mustard -- Grey Poupon
1/2	teaspoon	white pepper
1	tablespoon	rice wine vinegar -- or pickle juice
1/2	teaspoon	dry dill weed -- or 1 1/2 tablespoons fresh, chopped
1/4	teaspoon	wasabi -- or to taste
5	cups	mayonnaise

After rough chopping the onions and pickles, place in a food processor and pulse until desired texture is gained. I like mine a small dice size, about 1/8 inch cube.

Whisk all other ingredients along with the mayonnaise in a large bowl; adjust seasonings. If desired, thin with small amount of pickle juice. Serve with any type of fish or seafood. This will keep for up to two weeks in the fridge. Serve with Hallo Bay Beer Batter Halibut, page 120.

A Whole Lotta - Teriyaki Sauce

Janet Hickok
Servings 75

20	ounces teriyaki sauce -- your favorite
1 1/2	cups Karo® syrup
3/4	cup honey
1	cup brown sugar
1 1/2	tablespoons sesame oil
1	tablespoon fish sauce -- optional
1/8	cup garlic -- minced
1	teaspoons chili oil
2	tablespoons fresh ginger root -- minced
1/2	tablespoon ground ginger -- optional
1/2	tablespoon onion powder
1	cup sesame seeds

Combine all ingredients and whisk well, making sure the sugar is completely dissolved. Place in jars and seal.

This is very concentrated and goes well with most any kind of meat. I've used it with grilled fish, beef, chicken, pork, onions, and to flavor white rice. This is a ridiculously large amount of sauce, but I have found that it disappears extremely fast at the lodge.

NOTE: I find it easier to divide the seeds amongst the jars and then pour the liquid on top. Shake well to combine.

Bean's Grill Rub

Bill Rediske
Yield 5 cups

12	tablespoons	Kosher salt
14	teaspoons	paprika
16	tablespoons	granulated garlic
16	tablespoons	sugar
24	tablespoons	ground cumin
5	tablespoons	dried thyme
6	tablespoons	ancho chile powder

Mix all in a large container until well blended.
Store in airtight containers. This goes especially well with all types of grilled red meat.
Rub generously all over cut of meat and let set for 30-60 minutes before grilling to your specifications.

Stupendous Seasoned Salt

Janet Hickok
Yield 4 1/2 cups

1	cup	celery salt
1	cup	garlic powder
1	cup	onion powder
1	cup	brown sugar -- or to taste
4	tablespoons	paprika
3	tablespoons	chili powder
1	tablespoon	pepper
1	teaspoon	cayenne
2	teaspoons	cumin

Mix ingredients together thoroughly. Add and subtract to your taste.
A general, all-purpose seasoning salt to be used for most anything.

Perfectly Delicious Pesto

Janet Hickok
Yield Approximately 2 cups

6	tablespoons pinenuts -- toasted lightly
6	bunches fresh basil leaves
10	cloves garlic -- or to taste
1 1/2	cups grated fresh Parmesan cheese -- or more if needed
1	cup olive oil -- or as needed
	Kosher or sea salt and fresh ground black pepper -- to taste

Place all but the oil and salt and pepper in the bowl of a processor and pulse until ground and well mixed. While machine is running, slowly add olive oil until smooth, creamy and desired consistency. Add salt and pepper to taste.
Use with Anytime Pesto-Pizza Bagels, page 3, or with any and all recipes that call for pesto.

Salsa de Silvia

Silvia Ruiz
Servings 8

8	whole tomatoes -- chopped
8	jalapenos -- cored, seeded, minced - use gloves
1/2	bunch cilantro -- chopped
1	pinch Kosher or sea salt -- or to taste

Combine tomatoes and jalapenos (6 jalapenos is mild, you may use up to 16, I use 8) and place in a saucepan. Add small amount of salt and bring to a boil. Remove from heat, adjust salt to taste, add chopped cilantro and store.

ASADA STYLE SALSA: Roast the tomatoes over open flame to blacken the skin and add another layer of flavor.
VERDE STYLE SALSA: Use tomatillos in place of tomatoes.
VERDE STYLE SALSA II: Use tomatillos, NO cilantro, RED chilis, and garlic.

Red Bandana BBQ Sauce

Janet Hickok
Yield 2 Gallons

1	pound bacon -- cut into pieces
8	cups onions -- chopped fine
8	cloves garlic -- minced
1	cup celery -- finely chopped, optional
114	ounces ketchup -- or 1 No. 10 size can
1 1/2	cups vinegar
1 1/2	cups fresh lemon juice -- or bottled RealLemon
4	cups Worcestershire sauce
1 1/2	cups light corn syrup
1 1/2	cups molasses
2	cups dark brown sugar
4	tablespoons cumin
4	teaspoons tabasco sauce
1	teaspoon oregano
8	teaspoons chili powder
8	teaspoons red pepper flakes -- or to taste
8	teaspoons paprika
6	teaspoons dry mustard
5	teaspoons salt -- adjust salt to your
4	tablespoons mustard seed -- optional
2	teaspoons liquid smoke flavoring -- optional

Fry bacon pieces, drain keeping just enough fat to saute onions,
celery and garlic. Add all other ingredients, except liquid smoke,
and simmer for at least 1 hour. Return bacon to pan and simmer
for at least one more hour. The longer you cook it, the more
concentrated the flavors and the deeper the taste. Be very careful
that it doesn't burn. There is a fairly high sugar content and as it
thickens it will need more stirring.

At this time you have the option of adding a slurry of 1/2 cup
cornstarch and 1/2 cup cold water whisked together to thicken
the sauce to your preference. This is optional and does not add
or diminish the look or flavor. Add liquid smoke, cook and stir for
15 minutes more.
I store in fridge in glass or plastic containers without metal lids.
Stores for 3-4 weeks in the fridge or can if desired.

Happy Halibut Seasoning

Janet Hickok
Yield Approximately 1 cup

2	tablespoons seasoned salt
6	tablespoons sesame seeds
2	teaspoons dried dill weed
1/2	teaspoon celery seed -- crushed
2	teaspoons red pepper flakes -- crushed
1	teaspoon garlic powder
4	teaspoons lemon pepper
4	teaspoons brown sugar, packed
6	tablespoons dry Parmesan cheese

Combine all ingredients and store in airtight container.
Use liberally by patting on fish fillets that have been rinsed and
patted dry and then lightly coated with olive oil. Sear on both sides
in a medium-hot pan with a small amount of olive oil or clarified
butter until the fish is just cooked and a golden crust is formed.

NOTE: Halibut is one type of fish that suffers greatly from being
overcooked. Practice will teach you when it is almost done and
the best time to remove it from the heat. It should be cooked just
until opaque and will flake easily yet the center is still slightly
translucent. Remember - residual heat will finish the cooking.

Pridgen's Cocktail Sauce

Jim Pridgen
Servings 9

10	ounces ketchup
4	ounces prepared hot shorseradish
1/3	cup Worcestershire sauce -- or to taste
1/3	cup lemon juice -- or to taste

Whisk all ingredients together until well blended. Adjust seasonings and heat to your taste.
Will keep in fridge for 2 weeks.

Dartmouth Marinade

Janet Hickok
Makes 4 cups

2	cups fresh orange juice
1/2	cup brown sugar
1/2	cup soy sauce
1	cup red wine vinegar
1/4	cup olive oil
4	scallions, minced
4	cloves garlic, minced fine
1	teaspoon red pepper flakes, or to taste
1	teaspoon freshly ground black pepper
1	tablespoon ground cumin
1	teaspoon fresh ginger, minced fine
6	ounces tomato paste
1 1/2	tablespoons pickling spice

Warm the orange juice in the microwave until almost boiling, approximately 2 minutes. Whisk in the sugar until well blended, smooth, and sugar has dissolved. Whisk in remainder of ingredients until well blended.

Use to cover fish and place in fridge to marinate for 6-8 hours or overnight. Grill, broil, or bake fish as desired.

This will keep for two weeks in the fridge. Goes well with chicken also.

Enriques Salsa Ranchero

Enrique Hinajosa
Makes 4 cups

1	cup onion, sliced
2	serrano peppers, seeded and sliced
1	tablespoon olive oil
2	cups tomatoes, chopped
1/2	cup chicken stock, or as needed
1/2	cup water, or as needed

Heat oil in a skillet and cook the onions and peppers until soft-ened. Add tomatoes, chicken stock and water. Cook until melded and reduced to desired consistency. May be blended for a smoother texture.

NOTE: The tomatoes, onions, and chile peppers may be grilled or charred over flame for a great, slightly different flavor.

Aubrey's Secret Salsa

Aubrey Sims
Servings 4

2	cans stewed tomatoes -- or Italian stewed tomatoes
1	jalapeno chile pepper -- or more if desired, minced fine
1	teaspoon sugar

Mix all together in blender. Adjust flavor with salt and pepper to taste.

Cioppino Seasoning Blend

Janet Hickok
Servings 36

2	teaspoons	celery seed
6	teaspoons	lemon pepper
6	teaspoons	thyme
6	teaspoons	basil
6	teaspoons	Kosher salt
6	teaspoons	parsley
3	teaspoons	ground oregano
3/8	teaspoon	cayenne pepper
4	whole	bay leaves -- ground

Grind bay leaves in an electric grinder and combine with other ingredients to make the seasoning blend. Use approximately 1/2 - 1 teaspoon of seasoning per serving of cioppino soup, or to taste. Store in a glass or plastic, sealable container. Use with Hallo Bay Seafood Cioppino, page 51.

Viva La Guacamole

Janet Hickok
Servings 6

2	large	avocados -- peeled and seeded
1	tablespoon	lime juice
2	tablespoons	onions -- finely grated
1	tablespoon	cilantro -- chopped fine
1/8	teaspoon	tabasco sauce -- or jalapeno sauce
1/2	teaspoon	Kosher salt
1		tomato -- seeded and chopped fine

Coarsely mash the avocadoes and fold in the remaining ingredients. Make just prior to serving or place in zip top plastic bag with all the air removed and chill. If you would like this to be truly authentic, the tomato and salt are left out of the mix. Spread guacamole in a bowl, sprinkle with the salt and top with the tomatoes. This seals the guacamole and prevents it from turning dark. Serve with tortilla chips.

111

114

Entrees

Ginger-Scallion Butter for Salmon

Janet Hickok
Servings 16

2	sticks soft butter
2	tablespoons honey
1	tablespoon minced ginger -- or to taste
4	scallions -- minced
1/4	teaspoon garlic salt -- or to taste
1	pinch white pepper

Whisk all ingredients together until very well blended.

NOTE: I soften my butter in the microwave. Start with 1 minute at power level 3 (or defrost) and continue for 30 second intervals until butter is very soft but still holding its shape.

Rinse salmon, remove bones and pat dry. Set aside.
Arrange fish, flesh side down, on a heated and oiled grill.

Cook salmon 7 minutes. Turn and cook 5 minutes, or until salmon is just cooked through. Generally, salmon is cooked for 10 minutes an inch (at thickest point) at 400 degrees. This is a starting point, you need the flesh to just come to or pass the transluscent point. An easy way to check is to insert a sharp knife into the thickest part of the flesh and hold for 30 seconds. Remove and carefully hold the tip of the knife to your lips. The heat you feel is the heat of the fish and is done when is feels very warm but not super hot.
Just before serving, top with Ginger-Scallion Butter and sprinkle with toasted sesame seeds and green onions to garnish. If desired This can be used with any kind of salmon. It is also good with other kinds of fish, such as snapper, tuna, or halibut.

Herbalicious Basil Beurre Blanc

Janet Hickok
Servings 18

1/3	cup shallots -- minced
2	teaspoons butter
2/3	cup dry white wine
1	medium lemon -- juiced
1/4	cup white wine vinegar
15	tablespoons unsalted butter -- cut in pieces
1/2	cup fresh basil -- julienned
	Kosher or sea salt -- to taste

Over medium-high heat, combine shallots and 2 teaspoons butter and saute for 2 minutes. Add wine and lemon juice.
Cook uncovered until shallots are tender and liquid is almost gone, about 12 minutes. Remove from heat and whisk in butter, one piece at a time, until sauce becomes thick and glossy. Keep warm in a thermos or on very, very low heat. Serve over grilled or poached salmon.

NOTE: The above method is the traditional way of making a butter sauce. I have found that this is slow and tedious and completely unnecessary.
When it comes time to add the butter, instead of whisking in one piece at a time, place all of the butter in a glass bowl and microwave on power 3 for one minute and then for 30 second increments until the butter is "pudding soft" but still holding its shape. Stir your shallot mix into this, salt to taste and add the herb of your choice. Basil is great but so are fresh dill, tarragon, saffron, etc. Experiment with all kinds of flavors and enjoy. Serve with grilled fish cooked as described in previous recipe, page 118.

Hallo Bay Beer-Batter Halibut

Janet Hickok
Servings 24

5	cups	buttermilk pancake mix -- I prefer Krusteaz ® brand
36	ounces	beer -- flattened
1	tablespoon	lemon pepper
2	teaspoons	dill weed -- dried
12	pounds	halibut

Remove skin from halibut and cut into 1" cubes. If the halibut has been frozen for any length of time (3 months or more), place in a bowl and cover with milk. This step will bring back the "sweetness" of fresh halibut. Let set in refrigerator for at least 4 hours.

Place dry ingredients in a large bowl and pour in flattened beer and seasonings, then whisk until well combined.

Heat peanut or vegetable oil to 375 degrees.

Dip halibut pieces in batter and drop into hot oil and cook for 1 to 1 1/2 minutes, or until golden. Do not overcook! Drain well and serve with Onion-Dill and Pickle Tarter Sauce, page 100.

NOTE: Flat beer is required so that the yeast in the beer does not leaven the batter and make it cook up thick and cakey. To flatten the beer, simply open the can/bottles 3 or 4 hours early and let set, or pour into a pitcher and stir vigorously until the foam and suds no longer form.

NOTE: Experiment with different types of beers. You will get quite distinct variances in flavors. I prefer the lighter bodied beers, but the stouts and heavier beers may suit your taste.

Silver Salmon and Tomato Tartlets

Janet Hickok
Servings 6

3	tablespoons olive oil -- plus 1/3 cup
1/2	cup onion -- chopped fine
4	cloves garlic -- minced
3 1/2	cups plum tomatoes -- seeded and chopped, drained in a sieve
3	sage leaves -- chopped fine
1	sprig rosemary
2	each frozen puff pastry sheets
6	medium plum tomatoes -- cut 1/4" thick
12	ounces silver salmon -- cooked and flaked
1/2	cup freshly grated parmesan or romano cheese
2	tablespoons fresh basil -- minced

Heat 2 tablespoons oil in heavy medium skillet over medium heat. Add chopped onion and half of the minced garlic cloves; saute until translucent, 5 minutes. Add chopped tomatoes, sage leaves and rosemary sprig to skillet. Simmer tomato mix until reduced to 1 1/2 cups thick puree, about 30 minutes; remove herbs. Set aside.

Preheat oven to 425 degrees. Roll out 1 pastry sheet to thickness of 1/8 inch. Using a 7" plate as a guide, cut out 3 rounds. Repeat with other sheet, forming 6 rounds. Place three each on 2 large foil lined rimmed baking sheets.

Spread generous 2 tablespoons tomato puree over each round of pastry, leaving 1/2" around edge. Arrange tomato slices and salmon over puree; sprinkle with cheese, salt and pepper. Bake until tart crusts are golden, about 15 minutes.

Drizzle with remaining olive oil and sprinkle with fresh basil and return to oven for 6 minutes more. Remove from oven and let set for 10 minutes before serving.

Herbed King Salmon Bake

Janet Hickok
Servings 4

1 1/2	pounds	King Salmon fillet
1/2	cup	mayonnaise
2	tablespoons	sour cream
4	ounces	cream cheese -- softened
1/2	teaspoon	sugar
3	ounces	grated fresh Parmesan cheese
6	tablespoons	green onion -- minced
3	tablespoons	fresh herbs -- chopped
2	tablespoons	red bell pepper -- minced
1/2	lemon	-- juiced

Kosher or sea salt and fresh ground black
pepper -- to taste
Cayenne pepper -- to taste

Preheat oven to 350 degrees.
Spray foil-lined shallow baking pan with nonstick cooking spray
and warm in oven for 20 minutes.

Meanwhile, mix mayonnaise, sour cream, cream cheese, sugar,
parmesan, green onions, herbs (your choice, I prefer dill and
basill), bell pepper, lemon juice, salt, pepper, and cayenne in a
small bowl. Spread over flesh side of salmon fillet to within 1/2-inch
of edges.

Place salmon, skin side down, on heated pan (it should sizzle).
Bake 20 minutes or until just flaky. Do not overcook. Salmon
should be medium-rare to medium.

NOTE: See page 118 for salmon cooking guidelines.

Glazed-Grilled Salmon Steaks

Janet Hickok
Servings 4

6	tablespoons dark brown sugar -- packed
2	tablespoons honey
4	teaspoons mustard powder -- or dijon mustard
2	tablespoons soy sauce
2	teaspoons blasamic vinegar
4	16 ounce salmon steaks -- about 3/4" thick skin removed

Prepare grill.

Combine brown sugar, honey, mustard, and soy sauce in a medium bowl; whisk to blend.
Transfer 2 tablespoons glaze to small bowl; mix in the vinegar and set this portion aside to pass with the cooked salmon.

Brush skinned side of salmon generously with half of glaze. Place fish, glaze side down, onto hot grill. Cook until glaze is slightly charred, about 4 minutes. Brush top side of salmon with remaining glaze and turn over and grill second side until slightly charred and salmon is just opaque in center, about 5 minutes longer.
Transfer to a warmed platter and drizzle reserved glaze over salmon and serve.

V's Stroganoff

Vivian Hickok
Servings 6

1	tablespoon flour
1/2	teaspoon salt
1	pound beef -- cut into thin strips
2	tablespoons butter
3	ounces fresh mushrooms -- sliced
1/2	cup onions -- diced
1	clove garlic -- minced
2	tablespoons butter
3	tablespoons flour
1	tablespoon tomato paste
12	ounces beef broth
1	cup sour cream
2	tablespoons dry white wine

Combine first two ingredients and use to coat the beef. Fry in butter in a large skillet over medium-high heat until just pink. Add mushrooms, onions and garlic. Cook 3-4 minutes more. Remove meat mixture to a bowl and set aside. Keep warm.

In same skillet, melt 2 tablespoons butter. Add flour and stir for 2 minutes. Add tomato paste and broth. Cook, stirring until thickened and smooth, 5 minutes. Return meat to pan.

Fold in sour cream and wine. Do NOT boil! Serve over pasta or rice.

NOTE: Add a small amount of flour (1-2 teaspoons) to the sour cream to keep it from breaking/separating when heated. Be cautious about heating the dish too much or at too high a temperature after adding the sour cream.

Saffron, Shrimp, and Asparagus Penne Pasta

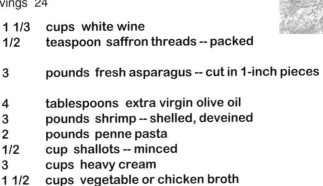

Janet Hickok
Servings 24

1 1/3	cups white wine
1/2	teaspoon saffron threads -- packed
3	pounds fresh asparagus -- cut in 1-inch pieces
4	tablespoons extra virgin olive oil
3	pounds shrimp -- shelled, deveined
2	pounds penne pasta
1/2	cup shallots -- minced
3	cups heavy cream
1 1/2	cups vegetable or chicken broth
1	teaspoon honey
	Kosher or sea salt and freshly ground pepper -- to taste

Combine saffron and wine; let steep for 20 minutes, set aside.
Bring a large pot of water to a boil and salt the water to taste.

In medium skillet bring about 1 inch of salted water to a boil. Add asparagus and cook for 3 minutes. Drain, plunge into ice cold water to stop the cooking process, drain well. Set aside.

Heat oil in a large pan, add shrimp and cook over medium-high heat, stirring, about 3 minutes. Transfer shrimp to a large bowl and keep warm.
Meanwhile put pasta into boiling water and cook according to package directions. Drain.
Place shallots and saffron/wine combo into just emptied pasta pan and bring to a boil over medium-high heat. Continue boiling until almost all the liquid is gone, 3 to 4 minutes. Stir in cream, vegetable or chicken broth, and honey; simmer over moderate heat until liquid is reduced by half. Stir in asparagus and shrimp.
Fold into cooked pasta. Heat through while gently stirring to blend shrimp. Heat through while gently stirring to blend ingredients. Adjust seasonings.

Pozzi's Naked Jaybirds

Bruce Pozzi
Servings 4

3 1/2	pounds	whole Cornish Game Hen
1	tablespoon	olive oil
1	teaspoon	Kosher or sea salt
2	tablespoons	dried tarragon
1/4	cup	water
1/2	cup	sugar

Pat chicken dry with paper towels. Twist wing tips to the back; tie legs and tail together. Rub chicken with the oil and sprinkle with the salt. Put tarragon in the center of a 24-inch length of 18-inch wide, heavy duty foil; pour the water (it won't spread too far) over the tarragon and place the chicken over the herb and water. Bring opposite sides of the foil over the chicken so edges meet; crimp and fold; seal ends.

Place the foil package on the grid of a charcoal cooker about 5 to 6 inches from medium-hot coals; cover grill and cook chicken until tender, about 30 to 40 minutes. Remove package from grill and let stand about 10 minutes. Save the juices from the package for a sauce or some other use if desired.

Shape a pan from heavy duty foil about 1 inch longer than the chicken to catch drippings.

With tongs and a barbecue mitt, carefully remove the grid of the grill; place the foil pan directly on the coals. Sprinkle the sugar over the bottom of the pan. Replace the grid; place the chicken, removed from the foil packet, directly on the grid over the foil pan of sugar. Cover grill; cook until chicken is evenly and well browned, about 10-15 minutes. The sugar burns and gives the chicken color and flavor. Serve hot or cold.

Lazy Dayz Texas Brisket and Dry Rub

Janet Hickok
Servings 25

1	tablespoon garlic powder
8	tablespoons chili powder
2	tablespoons paprika
4	tablespoons Kosher or sea salt
4	tablespoons cumin seed -- toasted and ground
4	teaspoons oregano
4	teaspoons sage
2	teaspoons cayenne
2	teaspoons black pepper
1/2	cup brown sugar
1/2	cup sugar
2	brisket, lean -- about 10 pounds each

Mix first eleven (dry) ingredients together well and rub into two 10-12 pound briskets. This may make more rub than you'll use; store remainder in airtight container.

Place briskets fat side up on double layer of foil large enough to completely surround meat and wrap very tightly.
Place in a shallow roasting pan.

Bake at 255 degrees for at least 8 hours. Meat should be very tender and falling apart. Slice to serve, removing excess fat.

Serve with warmed Red Bandana BBQ Sauce, page 104.

Entrees

Picante-Pesto Pasta

Janet Hickok
Servings 6

2	cups spinach -- firmly packed
1/2	cup fresh basil leaves, packed
1	cup picante sauce -- homemade or bought
1/2	cup parmesan cheese -- grated
1/2	cup pine nuts, toasted
1/3	cup vegetable oil
1	clove garlic -- minced
1	cup chicken broth -- or more if needed
1	pound pasta, fettuccine or linguine

Combine spinach, basil, 1/4 cup of the picante sauce, cheese, pinenuts, oil and garlic in a processor. Pulse until smooth. Transfer to a bowl; add remaining sauce and chicken broth. Cook pasta to al dente according to the directions on the package. Drain. Toss with picante-pesto sauce. If more liquid is needed add chicken broth to your taste.

Picadillo Sanchez

Natalia from Laredo

3	pounds lean ground beef
4	serrano peppers -- with stems
2	cloves garlic
1	teaspoon whole black peppercorns
1 1/2	teaspoons cumin seed
1/2	large onion -- sliced lengthwise
8	ounces tomato sauce
1 1/2	cups water

Brown beef in a dutch oven, salt and pepper lightly. When just beginning to brown, add onion and whole chiles and let simmer until they are starting to soften. Meanwhile, in a molcajete or mortar and pestle, crush the peppercorns, cumin seeds and garlic until finely mashed. Add a small amount of water to collect the spices and pour into the beef mix. Stir in tomato sauce and the water and let simmer on medium heat for 15-20 minutes. Serve with fresh flour tortillas, page 14.

Honey-Thyme Grilled Chops

Janet Hickok
Servings 24

1	cup honey
1	tablespoon garlic salt -- or to taste
1	cup butter
1	tablespoon balsamic vinegar -- preferably white
1 1/2	teaspoons fresh -- or 1 teaspoon dried thyme
24	pork chops -- cut 1 to 1 1/2 inch thick

Combine all ingredients and melt together in the microwave for about 1 minute. Stir well to combine. Let set for at least 30 minutes for the flavors to blend. Reheat if necessary.

Light a grill and bring to medium-high heat. Cook pork chops on one side for about 10 minutes. Turn and baste with honey-thyme mix and cook until just done, another 10-12 minutes. Slather with more baste just before serving.

Wallburg Marinade

Molly Hedgecock
Makes 4 1/2 cups

1 1/2	cups vegetable oil
3/4	cup soy sauce
1/4	cup worcestershire sauce
1/3	cup lemon juice
1 1/2	cups red wine vinegar
2	cloves garlic -- minced
2	teaspoons dry mustard
2 1/4	teaspoons Kosher salt
1	teaspoon black pepper
1 1/2	teaspoons parsley, freeze-dried

MIx ingredients very well and use to marinate chicken breasts for 4-6 hours.
Grill over medium heat for 30 minutes.
NOTE: Use for fish; marinate for 30 minutes. Try on pork as well.

Chipotle-Molasses Grilled Pork Tenderloin

Janet Hickok
Servings 6

2	tablespoons	chipotle chiles - canned
1	tablespoon	onion powder
1/2	teaspoon	celery salt
2	cloves	garlic -- minced
1/2	teaspoon	cumin -- ground
1	cup	molasses
3/4	cup	brown sugar
1/2	cup	Kosher or sea salt
1/4	teaspoon	cinnamon, optional
1/4	cup	fresh cilantro -- chopped, optional
3	pounds	pork tenderloin -- well trimmed

Mix together the chipotle chilies, onion powder, celery salt, garlic, cumin, molasses, brown sugar, salt and cinnamon.

Place pork in a large plastic bag and pour marinade mix into bag. Remove all the excess air from the bag so the ingredients are touching meat on all sides. Chill at least 4 hours or overnight.

Prepare grill. Remove pork from marinade. Grill pork until brown on all sides, turning often, about 15-20 minutes. Cover and cook, for another 5-10 minutes, or until meat thermometer registers 145 degrees. Tent with foil for 5-10 minutes to let meat set. Slice and serve.

NOTE: If you can find a chipotle paste in the ethnic section of your grocery store, I think you will find it to be as good or even better than the canned whole chiles.

Wonderful Wasabi Cream

Janet Hickok
Servings 16

2	whole shallots -- minced
2	tablespoons butter
1	clove garlic -- sliced
1 1/2	cups white wine

4	cups heavy whipping cream
3	tablespoons wasabi -- or to taste
	Kosher or sea salt -- to taste

In a heavy, medium-sized saucepan over medium heat, saute the shallots in the butter. After 2 minutes, add garlic and cook another 2 minutes. Remove garlic slices and increase heat to medium-high. Add white wine and boil until reduced to 1/2 cup.

Add whipping cream and return to a boil, reducing by half to approximately 2 cups. Watch this step carefully until cream comes to a full rolling boil. Then adjust heat so that cream continues to simmer vigorously, but won't boil over.

Whisk wasabi paste into cream reduction and season with salt to taste. Keep warm and use to pour over scallops, salmon, tuna, beef, or, use as a fantastic pasta sauce.

Chicken Curry Ka-Pow!

Kylee Hickok
Servings 12

1	tablespoon	vegetable oil
6	cloves	garlic -- minced
3		jalapenos -- seeded and minced

1 1/2	cups	coconut milk -- canned
1/3	cup	peanut butter, creamy
1/3	cup	soy sauce
2	tablespoons	fresh lime juice
2	tablespoons	sesame oil
2	tablespoons	fresh ginger -- peeled and minced
1	tablespoon	brown sugar
1 1/2	teaspoons	hot pepper sauce -- optional
2	tablespoons	curry paste -- or to taste. I use Pataks ®

1	pound	linguine

2	tablespoons	vegetable oil
1 1/2	pounds	chicken breast, no skin, no bone -- cut into 1/4" strips

1	tablespoon	vegetable oil
3/4	cup	green bell peppers -- diced
3/4	cup	red bell pepper -- diced
1/2	cup	mushrooms -- sliced
1/2	cup	green onions -- chopped

2	tablespoons	fresh basil -- julienned

Heat one tablespoon oil in a large heavy saucepan over medium heat. Add garlic and jalapenos, saute until tender, but not brown, about 3 minutes. Add coconut milk, peanut butter, soy sauce, lime juice, sesame oil, ginger, brown sugar, hot pepper sauce, and curry paste; whisk until smooth. Bring all to a simmer. Remove from heat. Season with salt and pepper to taste.
Cook linguine according to box directions, or until tender but still

firm to the bite. Stir occasionally and drain well when done.

Saute chicken strips in 1 to 2 tablespoons of oil until lightly browned and just cooked through.

Meanwhile, heat remaining tablespoon of oil in large heavy skillet, over medium-high heat. Add bell peppers, mushrooms, green onions and saute for 3 minutes. Add chicken and saute until cooked through. Combine sauce with the chicken/vegetable mixture and pour over pasta; toss well to coat. Fold in basil.

This recipe is easy and fairly quick and is also very delicious with shrimp or scallops in place of, or along with, the chicken. Any combination of vegetables that you like also works well.

Cranberry Chicken

Mary Ann Houtz
Servings 6

12	chicken breast halves
16	ounces catalina dressing
1	package french onion soup mix
1	can whole berry cranberry sauce

Preheat oven to 350 degrees. Grease a glass 9x13 inch baking dish and arrange breast pieces with skin up.

Combine dressing, soup mix and cranberry sauce and pour over chicken.
Bake for 1 hour.

NOTE: This recipe is more delicious than it sounds.

Apple-Wine Baked Chicken

Bubba Woods' Mother
Servings 18

24	pieces chicken thighs
	Kosher or sea salt and fresh ground black pepper -- to taste

2	cups apple juice
2	medium apples -- sliced
1	cup white wine -- or sherry
1/2	cup butter -- cut into pieces
1	tablespoon fresh herbs -- minced, your choice

Preheat oven to 450 degrees.

Place chicken pieces, skin side up, in a glass baking dish. Salt and pepper to taste. Bake chicken 20 minutes or until browned. Remove chicken from oven and reduce heat to 350 degrees.

Drain off accumulated fat and juices; add apple juice to chicken in baking dish and cover with foil and bake for 1 hour.
Add wine, apple slices, butter pieces, herbs and return to oven, uncovered, for 1 hour more. Baste every 10 minutes.

Note: The original recipe calls for dove or quail and it had them floured, seasoned, and pan fried before placing in the oven. I have taken the liberty of changing the recipe for ease and reduction of fat. I have also used this excellent recipe for game hen, ptarmigan, and duck with excellent results. I have grilled the birds, as the pre-cooking step, and like that as well. It is obvious that this recipe is adaptable. So, choose the fresh herbs, (I recommend sage, thyme and/or rosemary sprigs) wine, and juices of choice.

Silky Citrus Cream Pasta Sauce

Janet Hickok
Serfvings 8

8	tablespoons butter
1	clove garlic -- minced
3	large lemon -- zested and juiced
1	cup chicken stock
1	cup whipping cream
1/2	teaspoon sugar
3/4	pound linguine -- or other pasta
1/2	cup fresh parsley -- chopped
3/4	cup parmesan cheese -- freshly grated

Melt butter in large skillet over medium-low heat and add garlic, cooking for 1 minute. Add lemon juice and chicken stock and bring to a boil. Allow to reduce by one third. Whisk in whipping cream, return to a boil and reduce by another third. Reduce heat to a simmer. Add zest and sugar; cook for 5 minutes more. Remove from heat. (Can be prepared up to one hour ahead, keep warm.)

Cook pasta in large pot of boiling, salted water until tender but still firm to bite. Drain well. Add pasta, lemon zest and parsley to sauce. Toss together over medium heat to coat. Adjust seasoning to taste with salt and pepper. Sprinkle pasta with parmesan cheese and serve.

NOTE: This pasta sauce is elegant, easy and delicious. It goes well with any kind of seafood, chicken, and vegetables. Try using it with your favorites.

Seafood Paella de Madrid

Janet Hickok
Servings 8

1	teaspoon whole black peppercorns
1/2	teaspoon cumin seed
1/2	teaspoon minced fresh rosemary
4	cups chicken stock
1	pinch saffron threads, or to taste
1/4	cup olive oil
2	cloves garlic, sliced
1/2	medium onion, sliced lengthwise
2	cups rice
2	each red and green bell peppers, sliced lengthwise
1	cup peas, frozen
8	stalks asparagus, trimmed
16	shrimp
16	scallops, small

In a small skillet over medium-high heat, toast the peppercorns and cumin seed until fragrant and lightly browned, 1-2 minutes. Combine with the rosemary in a coffee grinder used exclusively for spices and grind into a coarse powder. Set aside.

Heat chicken stock in a saucepan or in the microwave and add the saffron threads to steep for 10 minutes. Set aside.

In a paella pan or heavy duty, large skillet, heat the olive oil until shimmering; add garlic slices and cook while stirring until fragrant and lightly browned, 2 minutes. Remove garlic. Lower heat to medium and add the onions and rice. Stir continuously until onion is translucent and rice is toasty brown. Add chicken stock and spice mix; stir to combine. Cover and lower heat to medium-low. Let cook for 12 minutes.

Attractively distribute the bell peppers around pan. Cover and cook 5 minutes more. Arrange the peas, asparagus, shrimp and scallops around pan. Cover and cook for 8 minutes more or until all the stock is evaporated and the rice is cooked through.

I learned this recipe from a gentleman that was originally from

Spain and was told that the traditional paella is cooked over an open fire and is infused with a wonderful smokey flavor. He said that there were usually snails in the dish and that the rosemary approximates their flavor. He also said that chicken and pork were never mixed with seafood. It was always a seafood paella with fish, scallops, shrimp, calamari, clams, and mussels - or with other meats including chicken, pork, chorizo or a hard Spanish sausage.

Creamy Broccoli-Chicken Casserole

Janet Hickok
Servings 18

8	chicken breast halves without skin
2	pounds frozen broccoli flowerets, thawed and drained
1	cup mayonnaise
1	cup sour cream
1	can cream of mushroom soup, condensed
1	teaspoon honey
1/2	teaspoon sage
1/8	teaspoon each Kosher salt and black pepper
2 1/2	cups shredded cheddar cheese, for topping
2 1/2	cups crushed cheese crackers, or potato chips, for topping

Preheat oven to 350 degrees. Saute the chicken until the juices run clear. Distributre the chicken evenly over the bottom of a 9x13 inch baking pan.

Place broccoli in a sieve; drain completely . Press on it with paper towels to aid in the water removal. Spread over chicken in pan.

Whisk remaining ingredients (except for toppings) together until well blended. Spread over broccoli and chicken. Bake for 45 minutes. Top with the cheese; return to oven for 8 minutes. Top with crackers or chips and return to oven to brown slightly, 8-10 minutes or until golden. Let set for 15 minutes before serving.

Chicken and Black Bean Enchiladas

Janet Hickok
Servings 18

5	pounds boneless chicken breasts -- cut into strips
12	slices bacon
8	cloves garlic -- minced
5	cups Salsa de Silvia, page 103
1/2	cup tomato paste
64	ounces black beans -- undrained
4	red bell peppers -- diced
4	teaspoons cumin
1	teaspoon salt
1 1/3	cups green onions -- sliced
6	cups Monterey Jack cheese -- shredded
18	flour tortillas
2	cups sour cream
3	avocados, sliced
3	limes, cut into wedges

Cook bacon, drain and crumble.
Cook and stir chicken and garlic in small amount of bacon fat, until just cooked through in center, about 10 minutes. Stir in 2 cups of the salsa, tomato paste, beans, peppers, cumin and salt. Simmer for 15 minutes until slightly thickened. Stir in the onions and bacon.
Preheat oven to 350 degrees.
Fill tortillas with the hot mix, approximately 1/4 to 1/2 cup per tortilla. Place a tablespoon of cheese on top of mix and roll. Place in a lightly greased 9x13 inch pan. Top with remainder of salsa.

Bake for 15 minutes or until heated through. Top with remaining cheese and return to oven until melted.

Serve with sour cream, avocados and lime wedges if desired.

Korean Style Grilled Beef Short Ribs

Janet Hickok
Servings 18

5	cups soy sauce
2	cups sugar -- I use 1 cup white and 1 cup brown
1/4	cup sesame oil
3	tablespoons garlic -- minced
3	bunches green onions -- finely chopped
3	tablespoons fresh ginger root -- peeled, minced
1	teaspoon salt, optional
6-9	pounds of beef short or cross cut ribs

Whisk together all ingredients until sugar is completely and thoroughly dissolved. Place in a large, zip-top plastic bag along with the meat and let marinate for at least 4 hours or overnight.

Preheat grill. Cook ribs until browned and charred on one side, about 10 minutes, depending on thickeness of the cut; flip and grill another 5-6 minutes.

Beef Tenderloin Weber

Louie Weber
Servings 20

1	cup molasses -- or as needed
1/2	cup Kosher or sea salt
1/4	cup peppercorns -- 3 blend, crushed
1	tablespoon herb of choice, such as rosemary, thyme or tarragon

Coat meat with molasses and then roll to coat in salt, crushed peppercorns and herbs.
Grill on highest heat for 15-20 minutes. Remove from heat and let set for 20-30 minutes and then return to grill and finish over indirect heat to desired doneness.

Guatemalan Grilled Shrimp and Vegetable "Martini"

Janet Hickok
Servings 20

2	whole red bell peppers, chopped
2	whole green bell peppers, chopped
2	whole yellow bell peppers, chopped
2	large sweet onion, chopped
32	fluid ounces crushed tomatoes
2	tablespoons ketchup
2/3	cup chopped fresh cilantro
2	tablespoons fresh lime juice
1/2	teaspoon Kosher salt
1/4	teaspoon fresh ground black pepper
2	pounds shrimp, peeled and deveined
4	large tomatoes, chopped
8	green onions, whole, chopped
4	avocado, chopped

Prepare grill on high heat. Char the peppers, onion and tomatoes until slightly blackened and softened. Grill the shrimp until just pink. Keep separate and set both aside.

Combine the charred vegetables along with the ketchup, cilantro, lime juice, salt and pepper to taste in a blender or food processor and blend until smooth.

To the blended mix add the grilled shrimp, chopped tomatoes, green onions, and avocadoes and toss together.
Serve in martini or margarita glasses and pass tortilla chips, or as the South Americans would, with saltine crackers.

NOTE: I love this combination of flavors so well, that I eat it cold and hot. It makes a great dip and a great topping for pasta or thinned with more tomato juice as a filling and fantastic soup.

Scotch Sugar-Grilled Sockeye Salmon

Janet Hickok
Servings 6

3	medium salmon fillets
1/2	cup butter
1/2	cup brown sugar
2	teaspoons sweet onion -- grated
1	teaspoon garlic powder
1/4	teaspoon yellow mustard seed
1/4	teaspoon celery salt
1/2	teaspoon Kosher salt -- or to taste
1/2	teaspoon fresh ground black pepper -- or to taste
1/2	large lemon

In a small but heavy saucepan, combine the butter, brown sugar, grated onion, mustard seed, garlic powder and celery salt. Place over high heat and whisk to mix well and to dissolve sugar. Bring to a rapid boil; contiunuing to boil for 5 minutes; careful not to boil over. Stir only once or twice. Taste; adjust seasonings to a perfect balance between salty and sweet.

Prepare grill and heat to high. Use indirect heat to cook salmon and place a foil drip pan under salmon when on grill.

Slather the flesh side of the fillets with a healthy portion of the scoth sugar mix. Carefully place fillets flesh side down directly on grill. Cook for 5-6 minutes. With a wide spatula very gently turn the fillets over and finish cooking skin side down, another 5-8 minutes. Baste with remainder of the scotch sugar mix. Just before serving squeeze lemon over top of salmon.

Tazimina River Wild Mushroom and Smoked Salmon Tart

Janet Hickok
Servings 16

1	cup	all-purpose flour
1/2	teaspoon	sugar
1/2	teaspoon	Kosher or sea salt
6	tablespoons	cold butter -- cut into chunks
1		egg yolk
2	tablespoons	sour cream
1/2	pound	mushrooms -- sliced, assorted wild
1/2	cup	smoked salmon -- broken up
4	tablespoons	unsalted butter
2	large	onions -- sliced
5	large	eggs
1 1/2	cups	heavy cream
1/4	teaspoon	Kosher or sea salt
1/4	teaspoon	white pepper
1/2	teaspoon	nutmeg
1/2	cup	shredded Parmesan cheese
1/2	cup	Swiss cheese
2	tablespoons	chopped fresh thyme
1	tablespoon	chopped fresh basil

TART SHELL: Preheat oven to 375 degrees. Mix the flour, sugar and salt together. Cut in the butter until the mix resembles cornmeal. Mix the yolk and sour cream together. Add to the flour mix and work together quickly until the pastry is well blended and will hold its shape. Press into a disc, cover with plastic wrap and chill for one hour.

Roll out the dough to 1/4" thickness and fit into a tart pan with a removable bottom. Fill with pie weights and bake for 10 mintues or until bottom is set. Remove weights and bake for an additional 5 mintues or until crust is light browned. Cool.

In a heavy skillet melt 2 tablespoons butter and add the sliced onions. Cook over low heat unitl the onions begin to brown. Set aside.

Preheat the oven to 350 degrees.
Beat the eggs and cream together; add salt, pepper and nutmeg to make a custard. Melt the remaining butter and set aside.

Spread the cooked onions on the baked pie/tart shell. Cover with grated cheeses, then spread with sliced mushrooms and smoked salmon; pour the custard over the top. Sprinkle with the chopped thyme and basil.

Bake for 25-30 minutes or until custard is set and the top is golden brown. During the baking, brush the top of pie/tart with remaining melted butter.

Allow to cool to room temperature and cut into 8 slices. May also be served warm to accompany any meat dish.

Spicy Creole Baked Shrimp

Janet Hickok
Servings 18

2/3	cup	olive oil
4	tablespoons	cajun seasoning
4	tablespoons	fresh lemon juice
4	tablespoons	fresh parsley -- chopped
1/2	cup	honey
2	tablespoons	soy sauce
1	pinch	red chili peppers -- or to taste
4	pounds	shrimp -- shelled, deveined

Combine first 7 ingredients in a glass bowl. Pour into a zip top plastic bag. Add shrimp and let set for 1 hour.
Preheat oven to 450 degrees and bake for 10 minutes stirring every 2-3 minutes; saute until just opaque.
Serve over pasta cooked al dente.

Grilled Chicken Enchiladas with Red Chile Sauce

Janet Hickok
Servings 4

1 1/2	tablespoons	corn oil
1	medium	onion -- chopped fine
1	tablespoon	garlic -- minced
3	tablespoons	chili powder
2	teaspoons	ground coriander
3	teaspoons	ground cumin
1/2	teaspoon	Kosher or sea salt
2	teaspoons	sugar
12	ounces	boneless skinless chicken breasts
16	ounces	tomato sauce
1	cup chicken broth	
1/2	cup	fresh cilantro leaves -- coarsely chopped
4	ounces	jalapeno peppers, canned -- drained and chopped

4   boneless, skinless chicken breast halves

4   cups grated cheddar cheese

8   each flour tortillas
         Vegetable cooking spray

1   cup grated cheese -- for accompaniment
3/4   cup sour cream -- for accompaniment
1   whole diced avocado -- for accompaniment
2   limes -- quartered

SAUCE AND FILLING: Heat oil in medium saucepan over medium-high heat until hot, 2 minutes. Add onion; cook, stirring occasionally, until softened and beginning to brown, 8 minutes. Add garlic, chili powder, coriander, cumin, salt, and sugar; cook, stirring constantly, until fragrant, 30 seconds. Add tomato sauce and 3/4 cup chicken broth. Bring to simmer, then reduce heat to medium-low; simmer uncovered, stirring occasionally, about 8 minutes. Add the cilantro, jalapenos, and set aside.

Grill chicken breasts on a preheated grill for 30 minutes or until golden brown and oozing clear juices. Remove from grill and let set for 15 minutes. Slice cooked chicken into long strips and place in a large bowl. Stir in half of the red chile sauce and half of the shredded cheese.

ASSEMBLE: Smear entire bottom of 9x13 baking dish with small amount of the chili sauce. Spray both sides of tortillas lightly with cooking spray. Increase oven to 400 degrees. Place 1/3 cup of the filling down center of each tortilla. Roll each tightly by hand and place in baking dish, side by side, seam side down. Pour remaining sauce over top of enchiladas. Use back of spoon to spread sauce so it coats top of each tortilla. Sprinkle 3/4 cup of grated cheese down center of the enchiladas. Cover dish with foil. Bake on lower-middle rack until heated through and cheese is melted, 20-25 minutes. Uncover and serve immediately, passing cheddar cheese, sour cream, avocado, lettuce and lime wedges separately.

Ancho Chili Pork Tenderloin

Janet Hickok
Servings 6

1	tablespoon	olive oil
1	teaspoon	ancho chile powder -- or to taste
1	medium	onion -- chopped fine
3	cloves	garlic -- minced
1	tablespoon	fresh ginger root -- peeled, minced
1	cup	chicken stock
1/2	teaspoon	ground cumin
1/2	cup	orange juice
1/4	cup	lime juice
1/4	cup	fresh cilantro -- chopped
2	tablespoons	orange peel -- grated
1	3 pound	pork loin -- well trimmed

Heat 1 tablespoon oil in a heavy skillet over medium heat. Add ancho chile powder, onion, garlic and ginger and saute until onion becomes soft, about 4 minutes. Add stock and cumin; simmer 5 minutes more. Transfer to a blender. Add orange juice, lime juice, cilantro and orange peel; process until smooth puree forms. Season with salt and pepper.

Place pork in a large zip top bag to marinate. Remove all the air and you can be sure that the liquid is touching the meat at all times. Rotate and turn once in a while. Pour puree over pork to coat. Cover and chill at least 4 hours or overnight.

Prepare grill to medium hot.

Remove pork from marinade and transfer liquid to a heavy saucepan and bring to a boil. Grill pork until brown on all sides, about 15-20 minutes, turning often or until meat thermometer registers 145 degrees. Brush often with marinade. Let meat set for 10 minutes. Slice and serve.

Shanghai Sweet and Sour Sauce

Janet Hickok
Servings 10

2/3	cup	red or white wine vinegar
1/8	cup	soy sauce
1/4	cup	sugar
1/4	cup	brown sugar
3/8	cup	ketchup
1/4	cup	Worcestershire sauce
1	teaspoon	salt
32	ounces	canned pineapple chunks
10		chicken breast halves
2		eggs
2	tablespoons	cornstarch
1/8	cup	cornstarch
1/4	cup	water
4	tablespoons	oil
1/2	tablespoon	crushed red pepper flakes
1	tablespoon	rice wine vinegar -- to moisten

Combine wine vinegar, soy, sugar, ketchup, worcestershire and salt. Set aside. Drain pineapple, set aside.
Cut up chicken (or, try with pork or seafood) and place in a zip-top bag; add in eggs and cornstarch; mush this around with your hands until well mixed and combined. Let set for at least 1 hour. Whisk cornstarch and water together to create a slurry.

Heat 1/2 of the oil on high heat and stir fry meat until just cooked through, set aside and keep warm.
Heat remaining oil, stir in garlic, do not let brown. Add your choice of fresh vegetables. I use green and red bell peppers and onions - chopped. Cook stirring for 3-4 minutes. When just tender crisp add red pepper flakes and meat. Moisten with rice wine vinegar. Add sauce and bring to a boil. Quickly stir in cornstarch slurry to thicken; cook for 2-3 minutes. Stir in pineapple and serve over rice.

Bacon Wrapped Grilled Ptarmigan Breasts

Janet Hickok
Servings 8

1	cup boiling water
2	tablespoons Kosher salt
2	tablespoons sugar
2	cups ice cold water
16	ptarmigan breast halves
2	cups boiling water
2	cups ice cold water
16	slices bacon
4	whole jalapeno chile peppers -- seeded and quartered
1	small onion -- cut into thin slivers
	Kosher salt and fresh ground black pepper -- to taste
2	cups boiling water
2	cups ice cold water

Bring one cup of water to a rolling boil in a 4-6 quart saucepan; add Kosher salt and sugar and stir until dissolved; add ice cold water to cool down for brining. Place breasts in brine for 1 hour to cleanse and flavor. Drain well on paper towels.

Bring another 2 cups of water to a rolling boil; add jalapeno pieces to boiling water and cook for 1 minute; add onion slices to pan and boil for 1 minute more. Drain; plunge immediately into ice cold water to stop cooking. Drain well. Set jalapeno/onion combo aside until needed. Clean ptarmigan breasts and carefully cut a small slit in the flesh to create a pocket. Insert one piece of onion and jalapeno into pocket and wrap breast with one slice of bacon; secure with a toothpick. Up to this point can be prepared one day ahead.

Heat and prepare grill. Grill over medium heat turning frequently until bacon is crisp and brown and ptarmigan is just barely pink inside - cut into one to check, about 20 minutes.

149

151

157

154

Sweets and Goodies

Triple Nirvana

Janet Hickok
Servings 24

1 1/2	cups	flour
3/4	cup	walnuts -- chopped
1/2	cup	butter -- melted
16	ounces	cream cheese -- soft
2	cups	powdered sugar
2	cups	whipped topping -- thawed in fridge
12	ounces	instant pudding mix -- chocolate, or your choice of flavor
3	cups	milk
1	teaspoon	vanilla

Preheat oven to 350 degrees.
Combine first 3 ingredients and press into the bottom of a 9x13 inch pan. Bake for 15 minutes. Cool completely.

Beat cream cheese until soft and smooth. Add powdered sugar and beat until smooth. Fold in cool whip and then spread evenly on cooled crust. Keep chilled.

Whip together pudding mix and milk until smooth; add vanilla. Spread as third layer on dessert. Chill until serving. At this point you may freeze and keep for several hours or up to 2 days. I like to freeze mine so that the entire dessert is firmer and much easier to cut. Remember to remove it and let it set in the refrigerator for about 2 hours before serving.
To serve, top with another layer of cool whip, cut into pieces and then sprinkle with additional nuts. Keep chilled until serving.

NOTE: This dessert is an all-time favorite that everyone loves and asks for repeatedly. It is extremely easy and can be found in many restaurants. I hesitate to give out the recipe because it is almost too simple to believe.
I have tried it with many different flavors of filling, but find that the chocolate, banana or coconut seem to go over the best. Also, I have used almonds or have left nuts out completely.

All America's Favorites - Frozen Peanut Butter Mousse Pie

Janet Hickok
Servings 20
Yield 2 pies

3	cups	Oreo ® cookies -- crushed fine
1/2	cup	butter -- melted
1	cup	Snickers ® candy bars -- crumbled
18	ounces	peanut butter -- creamy or crunchy
3/4	cup	powdered sugar
4	cups	heavy whipping cream
1/2	cup	Butterfinger ® candy bar -- crushed
8	ounces	chocolate syrup -- or as needed
8	ounces	caramel topping -- or as needed
		whipped topping -- optional

Stir finely crushed Oreo ® cookies and melted butter together until well mixed. Press into 2 pie pans and then sprinkle the crumbled pieces of Snickers ® bar over the crust. Set aside.

In an electric mixer bowl, with the beater attachment, beat the peanut butter and powdered sugar together until smooth and well blended. Add 1 cup of the whipping cream and mix on medium until the peanut butter mix is lightened. Scrape down sides. Mix in the remainder of the cream and beat until light and fluffy. Do not over mix as the cream will start to separate and "curdle". Fold in Butterfinger ® crumbles and turn out into pie shells. Place in freezer for at least 2 hours or until hardened.

Cut into 10 pieces and drizzle with the caramel and chocolate toppings. Add a dollop of whipped topping if desired.

Rhubarb Rush Crisp

Janet Hickok
Servings 12

1/2	cup	butter
1	cup	brown sugar
3/4	cup	sugar
1		egg
1	teaspoon	vanilla
1/2	teaspoon	salt
2 1/2	cups	flour
1	cup	sour cream
2 1/2	cups	rhubarb -- diced
1/4	cup	butter
1	cup	sugar
1	teaspoon	cinnamon

Preheat oven to 350 degrees.

Cream butter and sugars, add egg and vanilla. Combine flour
and salt; stir into creamed mix alternately with the sour cream.
Fold in rhubarb.

Blend chilled butter, sugar and cinnamon until crumbly, set aside.

Turn batter into a well buttered, 9x13 inch glass pan and sprinkle
with crumbled crisp topping.

Bake for 45 minutes or until a pick inserted in center comes out
clean.

Absolutely Incredible Ice Cream

Janet Hickok
Servings 24

3	**cups milk**
3/4	**teaspoon Kosher or sea salt**
1 1/2	**cups sugar -- divided**
9	**egg yolks**
3	**tablespoons vanilla**
6	**cups heavy cream**

In a heavy saucepan, combine the milk, salt and half of the sugar and whisk. Whisk constantly over medium until just reaching a boil, then remove from heat.

Meanwhile whisk the remaining sugar and yolks in a bowl until light and pale yellow. Temper the eggs by pouring the hot milk in very slowly while whisking constantly so that the eggs do not cook in clumps. Whisk until smooth; add the cold cream and the vanilla. Strain into an ice cream machine's container and chill for a couple hours. Process in ice cream machine according to the manufacturer's directions

This is my all-purpose, basic ice cream recipe. I use this as a base and then add all kinds of items to make specialty flavors. When making a chocolate based ice cream, I melt 8-12 ounces of chocolate in with the milk. Add any ingredients that appeal. I add mashed fruits, nuts, cookies, chocolate and candy pieces, flavorings (such as coffee, almond, lemon, coconut, citrus zests, etc.), cheesecake and cake pieces. Do not overload. Too much liquid, liquor or alcohol-based flavoring will inhibit proper freezing. Have fun and enjoy.

Chiller Key Limelets

Janet Hickok
Servings 16

4	cups	Oreos® -- crushed
1	stick	butter -- melted
3	cans	sweetened condensed milk
12	ounces	key lime juice
16	ounces	marshmallow cream
2	teaspoons	lime zest
1 1/2	pints	whipping cream
		lime slices -- for garnish

Combine melted butter and cookie crumbs and mix until evenly
coated. Press into two pie plates, tart pans or 16 individual tart
dishes.

In a clean, electric mixing bowl, whip the cream until firm peaks
form. Set aside and keep cold. In another large electric mixing
bowl, whip the sweetened condensed milk until it is thickened
and increased in volume. Add the lime juice and marshmallow
creamand continue mixing. It will thicken even more.
Fold in lime zest and a cup of the whipped cream to lighten the
lime mixture and then fold in remaining whipped cream. Turn out
into prepared crusts and freeze until 15 minutes before serving, at
least 4 hours. Garnish with additional whipped cream, lime slice
and/or mint leaves.

"MARGARITAS": I also use this recipe for a dramatic dessert
served in martini or margarita glasses that have been rimmed
with crystalized sugar that can be found in stores or online.
Ignore the crust section and fill the glasses with the lime mousse
mixture and freeze for at least 2-3 hours. Just before serving,
whip about 2 cups of heavy whipping cream until starting to
thicken and then add 1 tablespoon each of tequila and orange
flavored liqueur and 1/3 cup of sugar. Continue to whip until soft,
yet thick enough to flow over the tops of the frozen desserts.
Garnish with lime slices.

Black Jack Bread Pudding

Evelyn Kruse
Servings 12

5	**eggs**
3	**12 ounce cans evaporated milk**
2	**cups milk**
1 1/2	**cups sugar**
1/2	**cup butter -- melted**
2	**teaspoons cinnamon**
3	**teaspoons vanilla**
1	**teaspoon salt**
1	**cup raisins -- optional**
1	**loaf bread (1 lb) -- cut into 1/2" cubes**
1/2	**cup butter -- melted**
1	**cup brown sugar**
1/2	**cup cream**
2	**tablespoons bourbon whiskey**

Preheat oven to 350 degrees.

Whisk first eight ingredients together. Set aside.

Place bread and raisins into well buttered four-quart casserole.
Pour prepared custard mixture over it. Let set for 20 minutes.

Bake for 50-60 minutes or until pudding is lightly browned and
still has a slight "jiggle" to the center.

To make sauce, combine butter, brown sugar, cream and
bourbon (I like Jack Daniels ®) in a saucepan and bring to a boil.
Serve over bread pudding.

Can't Get Enough ~ Carrot Cake

Janet Hickok
Servings 20

2	cups flour
2	teaspoons baking soda
1/2	teaspoon salt
2	teaspoons cinnamon
1	pinch cloves, ground
3	large eggs
1	cup sugar
1	cup packed brown sugar
1	tablespoon honey
3/4	cup vegetable oil
3/4	cup buttermilk
2	teaspoons vanilla
2	cups carrots -- grated
8	ounces canned crushed pineapple -- drained
3 1/2	ounces coconut flakes
1	cup chopped walnuts -- or pecans
1	cup butter -- softened
12	ounces cream cheese -- softened
3	cups powdered sugar -- or as needed
1 1/2	teaspoons vanilla

Preheat oven to 350 degrees. Line three, 9-inch round, cake pans with parchment, lightly grease and flour pans, set aside.

Stir together first five (dry) ingredients. In an electric mixer bowl, beat eggs, sugars, honey, vegetable oil, buttermilk, and vanilla at medium speed until smooth. Add flour mixture and beat at low speed until blended. Fold in carrots, pineapple, coconut and nuts. Divide batter equally between prepared cake pans.

Bake for 25-30 minutes or until a toothpick inserted in center comes out clean.

Cool, in pans, on a wire rack for 15 minutes. Remove from pans and cool completely on wire racks.

I like to freeze my cake layers before assembling and frosting. It makes the process MUCH easier!!

FROSTING: Beat butter and cream cheese at medium speed, with an electric mixer, until creamy. Add powdered sugar and vanilla and beat until smooth. Frost between layers and on the top and sides of the cake.

Molly's Christmas Pound Cake

Molly Hedgecock
Servings 20

1	cup butter -- soft, (2 sticks)
3	cups sugar
6	whole eggs
1/4	teaspoon baking soda
1/2	pint sour cream
3	cups cake flour
1	teaspoon vanilla
1/2	teaspoon lemon juice

Preheat oven to 325 degrees.

Cream butter and sugar until light and fluffy. Add eggs one at a time, mixing between each. Stir soda into sour cream and then mix into batter alternately with the flour. Add flavorings and turn into a well greased and floured bundt pan.

Bake for 70-75 minutes. Let cool for 10 minutes and remove from pan onto a cooling rack.

Sweets and Goodies
Death By Chocolate

Janet Hickok
Servings 20

1	cup	water
1	cup	sugar
1	teaspoon	Kosher or sea salt
2	cups	butter
1 1/2	cups	semisweet chocolate chips
8	whole eggs	
2	teaspoons	vanilla

Preheat oven to 350 degrees.
Line a springform pan with foil (the batter is very thin and may leak without foil) and spray lightly with cooking oil. Using another piece of foil, wrap outside of springform pan. Set aside.

Place water, sugar, salt and butter in a heavy saucepan on medium-high heat and bring to a boil. Remove from heat and stir in chocolate until smooth. Add eggs, one at a time, beating well between each. Add vanilla and whisk together well. Strain into prepared pan. Make a hot water bath by placing the springform pan inside another, larger, pan and then fill the larger pan to half way up sides of springform with hot water.

Carefully place into oven and bake for 45-50 minutes. Cool for 20 minutes. Remove from water bath and cool for another 20 minutes. Cover and place in refrigerator and chill well before serving, at least 6 hours.

Top with your choice of chocolate, caramel or other type of sauce, fruit, jam/preserve, combination of, etc.

Creme Brulee Bliss

Janet Hickok
Servings 16

6	cups heavy cream
1/2	teaspoon Kosher or sea salt
15	egg yolks
1 1/2	cups sugar -- additional for topping
2	tablespoons vanilla
1 1/2	teaspoons flavored liqueur -- if desired

Preheat oven to 350 degrees.

Heat cream in heavy saucepan over medium, bringing just to the point of boiling. While cream is heating, beat yolks and sugar with electric mixer on low speed until pale yellow and thick ribbons form. Very slowly, temper yolks by gradually adding heated cream while whisking continuously. Stir in vanilla.
Strain mix into 6 ounce ramekins. Place ramekins in a shallow pan and add hot water (bain marie or water bath) to half way up dishes. Place in oven and bake for 45 minutes, or until set. Remove from hot water, and chill completely.
No more than 2 hours before serving, top each ramekin with 1 teaspoon sugar and spread evenly. Place under broiler until just melted. Return to refrigerator until ready to serve. Top with whipped cream or fresh fruit if desired.

NOTE: This will be one of the most spectacular and well received desserts you make, and, perhaps one of the easiest. I like to streamline and have found that by using the microwave and two large glass bowls, I can eliminate most of the time involved with the above instructions. Try this:
Place cream and salt in glass bowl and heat in microwave for 8-10 minutes. Watch carefully, it will suddenly come to the boiling point. Meanwhile whisk yolks and sugar together until light and creamy in a deep bowl. When cream is hot, pour approximately 1/2 cup into the eggs to temper them, whisk instantly and then add 1 cup more and whisk, and then combine completely.
Return to microwave for 3-4, one-minute intervals, stirring between each, until the custard begins to thicken. Add flavorings and follow directions for placing in ramekins and baking.

Lily's Wacky Cake

Lily Hickok
Servings 18

3	cups flour
2	cups sugar
2	teaspoons baking soda
2	teaspoons Kosher or sea salt
6	tablespoons unsweetened cocoa powder
2	teaspoons vanilla
2/3	cup vinegar
2	cups water
1/2	cup butter
2	tablespoons heavy cream
1	cup brown sugar
2	teaspoons vanilla
1 1/4	cups semisweet chocolate chips

Preheat oven to 350 degrees. Lightly spray a 9x13 inch pan with cooking spray.

Mix dry ingredients very well in a large bowl. Combine wet ingredients and pour into bowl. Fold together until all is moist. Pour into a prepared pan.

Bake for 25-30 minutes. Cool for 20 minutes.

FROSTING: Bring all ingredients except chocolate to a boil in a small saucepan over medium heat. Remove from heat and stir in chocolate until smooth.
Spread on cooled cake.

Butterscotch Banana Toffee Layer Tart with Animal Cracker Crust

Janet Hickok
Servings 20

1	cup heavy cream
1	cup butterscotch chips
3	cups animal crackers -- crumbs
1/2	stick butter -- melted
4	cups heavy cream
3	tablespoons butterscotch flavored schnapps
2	teaspoons vanilla
1/2	cup sugar
8	ounces instant vanilla pudding and pie filling
12	ounces caramel topping
6	large bananas -- sliced lengthwise
1	cup chocolate cookie crumbles
1	cup toffee -- pieces
1	cup caramel topping

Place cream and butterscotch chips in a glass measuring cup and heat in microwave for 2 minutes on high. Whisk together until smooth and melted.

MIx cookie crumbs and butter together and press into a 12 inch tart pan. Set aside.

In an electric mixer beat the cream, schnapps, vanilla, and butterscotch/cream mix together until soft peaks form. Add sugar and pudding; whisking on high unitl well combined and fluffy.

Drizzle caramel over crust and then layer in bananas. Sprinkle chocolate cookie crumbs over bananas. Pour whipped cream/pudding mix into crust; smoothing top. Freeze for 3-4 hours or until set and firm.

When ready to serve, cut into pieces and top with toffee and more caramel topping

NY Style Cheesecake

Janet Hickok
Servings 20

40	ounces cream cheese -- softened
1 1/2	cups sugar
2	eggs
3	egg yolks
1/4	cup flour
1/4	cup heavy cream
1/2	teaspoon vanilla
1	Pinch salt
1	lemon -- zested and juiced

Preheat oven to 400 degrees.

In a large mixer bowl combine cream cheese and sugar, mixing on low until well blended. Add eggs and yolks one at a time, mixing well between each. Add flour and mix well. Add cream and mix well. Turn mixer on high and beat for 5 minutes. Stir in vanilla, salt, and lemon juice.

Pour batter into a springform pan with a prepared crust.
(See NOTE:) Bake at 400 degrees for 20 minutes.(Do Not open oven door during cooking time) Turn oven down to 300 degrees and bake for 1 hour. Turn oven to 200 degrees and bake for 30 minutes and then turn oven off and leave in for another 30 minutes. Remove from oven and let set for 20-30 minutes or until cool. Cover with plastic wrap and place in fridge for at least 4 hours. Chill completely before attempting to cut. Try using fishing line to slice, it works unbelievably well.

NOTE: There are any number of flavorings that can be added to this recipe. Use your imagination. I have used melted chocolate, chopped or pureed fruit. I have added spiced pumpkin to the batter. I add orange juice concentrate or flavored liqueurs (both in small amounts). Spices, candies and nuts can also be used. Have fun and use this recipe as the starting point to many and varied delicious cheesecakes.

NOTE: I do not like graham cracker crusts and so here are a couple alternatives: 1 1/2 cups chocolate wafer cookies, crushed and 4 tablespoons melted butter and 1 tablespoon sugar. Mix and press into bottom of pan.
Or use a small box vanilla wafer type cookies, 1/2 cup melted butter, 1 cup pecans, 1/2 cup flour. Blend all in processor until fine crumbs. Press about 1 cup into bottom of greased springform pan. Freeze any leftover crumbs for next time. Bake for 8 minutes at 400 degrees. Let cool for 15 minutes before filling.

Tart Crust - The Very Best

Janet Hickok
Servings 12

1 1/4	cups all-purpose flour
1/3	cup powdered sugar
1/2	teaspoon Kosher or sea salt
10	tablespoons cold butter -- cut in small cubes
2	large egg yolks
1	tablespoon cold water

Mix flour, powdered sugar and salt in a food processor. Add butter, pulse until mix resembles coarse meal. Whisk yolks and water together and then add to flour mixture and pulse until moist clumps form. Gather dough into ball, flatten into disk. Wrap in plastic and chill 1 hour. Let dough soften slightly at room temperature before rolling out. Can be made up to 3 days ahead. Keep chilled or freeze.
This is a very soft dough and should be chilled until just prior to baking. Must be baked with a foil lining and pie weights so that dough will not slump in pan.
Bake at 350 degrees for 12 minutes, remove foil and pie weights and pierce all over with a fork to prevent bubbles from forming in dough. Bake for an additional 15 minutes.

This is my very favorite tart crust and may be used for both sweet and savory tarts. It has a rich, full flavor with a flaky, delicate crumb.

Poppy-Seed Cake with Orange-Almond Glaze

Janet Hickok
Servings 12

2 3/4	cups sugar
1	cup corn oil
3	whole eggs
1 1/2	teaspoons vanilla
1	teaspoon almond extract
3	cups flour
2	tablespoons poppy seeds
1 1/2	teaspoons baking powder
1/2	teaspoon salt
1 1/2	cups milk
1	cup powdered sugar
1/4	cup orange juice
1/4	teaspoon almond extract

Preheat oven to 350 degrees. Grease and flour a 9x13 inch pan.

In the bowl of an electric mixer, beat first 5 ingredients to blend.
Combine dry ingredients. Stir into sugar/oil mixture alternately with
milk.
Pour batter into prepared pan.

Bake for 50 minutes or until pick inserted in center of cake
comes out clean. Cool 10 minutes and then glaze.

GLAZE: Whisk together juice, sugar and flavoring until smooth
enough to spread over cake.

Foolproof Fudge Brownies

Genevieve and Bill Toupal, Stonewall CO
Servings 9

2	**eggs**
1	**cup sugar**
1/8	**teaspoon salt**
1	**teaspoon vanilla**
1/2	**cup butter or margarine**
2	**ounces unsweetened chocolate**
3/4	**cup flour**
1/2	**cup walnuts -- chopped**

Preheat oven to 350 degrees. Lightly grease an 8x8 inch baking pan; set aside.

Mix eggs, sugar, salt and vanilla together in a mixing bowl. Melt butter and chocolate together in a large glass bowl in the microwave. Cool slightly before stirring in egg mix. Add flour 1/2 cup at a time. Fold in nuts. Turn batter into baking pan. Bake for 30 minutes or less. Let cool for 20-30 minutes before cutting into squares.

I have doubled and tripled this recipe with no problems. Tripled fills a jelly roll pan nicely.

Memory Maker Bread Pudding

Janet Hickok
Servings 12

1	cup raisins -- optional
1/2	cup orange or almond flavored liqueur -- optional
2	cups milk
1 1/2	cups sugar
1	teaspoon Kosher salt
8	cups whipping cream
4	each whole eggs
8	each egg yolks
1	large loaf french bread -- cubed
1	tablespoon vanilla
1/8	teaspoon almond flavoring
1/8	teaspoon freshly ground nutmeg
1	teaspoon ground cinnamon

If using raisins and liqueurs, place raisins in a small saucepan along with the choice of flavors and bring to a simmer for 5 minutes. Shut off stove and let set until ready to use.

In a microwave proof bowl, heat milk for 3 minutes and then add the sugar and salt and whisk to dissolve completely. Whisk in cream, eggs, and egg yolks until completely combined. Add plumped raisins, their juices, vanilla and almond flavoring; stir well.

Place bread into a 9x13 inch baking pan - pour half of the cream/egg mixture over the bread and let set for 15 minutes and then top with rest of the cream/egg mix.

Cover loosely with foil and bake for 1 hour at 300 degrees. Remove foil and bake at 350 degrees for an additional 25 minutes until top is golden brown.

Serve warm or at room temperature. Top with warmed cream or half and half.

Rhubarb Crunch

Nelda Carlson
Servings 9

1	cup all-purpose flour
1	cup brown sugar
3/4	cup old-fashioned rolled oats
1/2	cup butter -- melted
1	teaspoon cinnamon
1	teaspoon Kosher or sea salt
4	cups rhubarb -- cleaned and sliced
1	cup sugar
1/2	teaspoon Kosher or sea salt
1	teaspoon vanilla
2	tablespoons cornstarch
1	cup water

In a medium bowl mix first five ingredients until well blended and then divide in half, and place half in a well greased 9x9 inch baking dish and reserve other half for topping. Place chopped frozen or fresh rhubarb in pan.

Preheat oven to 350 degrees.

In a small saucepan mix sugar, salt, cornstarch and water and whisk to combine. Bring to a boil, stirring frequently until thickened and bubbly. Pour over rhubarb and sprinkle with reserved topping.

Bake for 45-60 minutes. Serve warm or at room temperature with a generous scoop of homemade vanilla Absolutely Incredible Ice Cream, page 161.

Banana Flippin Eclairs

Janet Hickok
Servings 20

1	cup sugar
4	tablespoons corn starch
3 1/2	cups milk
4	large egg yolks -- lightly beaten
1	tablespoon butter
1	teaspoon vanilla
2	cups water
2	sticks butter
1/2	teaspoon Kosher salt
2	teaspoons sugar
2	cups flour
8	large eggs
5	large bananas
3	cups whipped cream
1 1/2	cups Real Hot Fudge Sauce, page 182

In a heavy medium saucepan combine the sugar and cornstarch and whisk to combine thoroughly. Stir in the milk. Cook over medium heat till bubbly. Cook and stir for 2 minutes more. Remove from heat. Carefully and slowly stir one cup of the milk mixture into the egg yolks to temper them without making scrambled eggs. Add rest of egg mix back into milk in saucepan and bring to a gentle boil. Reduce heat and cook and stir for 2 minutes more. Remove from heat. Stir in butter and vanilla. Pour into a bowl and place plastic directly on the pudding surface. Cool completely in fridge for 2-3 hours.

Preheat oven to 400 degrees.

In a medium saucepan combine water, butter, salt, and sugar. Bring to a boil. Add flour all at once, stirring vigorously. Cook and stir constantly until mix forms a ball; continue stirring and cooking for another minute. Remove from heat and place in the bowl of an

electric mixer. Turn on low and mix for 2 minutes, letting some of
the steam and heat escape. Add eggs, one at a time, beating well
after each addition until all are incorporated. Pipe dough onto a
parchment lined cookie sheet and bake for 30 to 35 minutes or
until dry and golden brown. Cut tops from puffs and remove any
excess dough. Fill puffs with 2-3 tablespoons of the pudding mix;
top with 1/4 of a banana; top with whipped cream. Replace top of
puff and drizzle with chocolate sauce.

World's Best Cookies

Molly Hedgecock
Yield 10 dozen

1	pound butter -- soft
2	cups brown sugar
2	cups sugar
1 1/2	cups vegetable oil
2	teaspoons vanilla
2	cups oats
2	cups corn flakes
2	cups coconut
1	cup pecans -- finely ground
5 1/2	cups flour
2	teaspoons soda
2	teaspoons salt

Preheat oven to 325 degrees.

Cream butter and sugars together. Slowly mix in oil and vanilla.
Add oats, cereal, coconut and pecans, mixing on low until just
combined. In another bowl, sift together the flour, soda and salt
and add to rest of the ingredients combining well. Chill; form into
balls.

Bake cookies for 12-15 minutes. Cool on rack and store in
airtight container or freeze.

Snowflake Sugar Cookies- They Melt In Your Mouth

Doris Hickok
Yield 10 dozen

2	cups	butter -- soft
2	cups	vegetable shortening
2	cups	sugar
2	cups	powdered sugar
4	eggs	
2 1/2	teaspoons	vanilla
2	teaspoons	soda
2	teaspoons	cream of tartar
8	cups	flour

Cream shortening, butter, and white sugar. Mix in powdered sugar. Stir in eggs and vanilla. Stir dry ingredients together in a separate bowl and mix in 1 cup at a time, scraping down sides of bowl as necessary.

Roll into logs by placing dough on waxed paper and rolling. Chill (or freeze) at this point. Slice into 3/8 inch slices when ready to bake.

Preheat oven to 350 degrees and bake for 8 minutes. Do not over bake these cookies. They should be very light and only just barely starting to "tan" on the edges. Cool on a wire rack.

Raisin-Oat-Nut Chews

Janet Hickok
Yield 10 dozen

2	cups brown sugar
1	cup sugar
1	cup vegetable shortening
1/2	cup butter -- softened
2	whole eggs
1/2	cup water
2	teaspoons vanilla
6	cups quick style oatmeal
2 1/2	cups flour
2	teaspoons salt
2	teaspoons cinnamon
1	teaspoon ground cloves
1	teaspoon soda
2	cups raisins
2	cups walnuts

Preheat oven to 375 degrees.
Cream shortening, butter and sugars until well blended and fluffed.
Add eggs, water and vanilla. Mix until just blended. Add oatmeal
and stir in. Combine dry ingredients and add in four batches,
mixing between each. Stir in raisins and nuts. Chill well before
forming into balls. Place 2 inches apart on parchment lined cookie
sheets.

Bake for 12-15 minutes. Cool on rack and then store in an
airtight container or freeze.

NOTE: Mix it up - add 1 cup chocolate or butterscotch chips,
dried cherries, dried blueberries, coconut, almonds, hazelnuts
etc. in place of, or in combination with, the raisins.

NOTE: John Tiernan recommends soaking the raisins in 1/2 to 3/4
cup of Myers ® dark rum overnight; drain and then use 1/4 cup of
water and 1/4 cup of the drained rum for the 1/2 cup of water in the
recipe. It is extraordinarily delicious.

Mother's Molasses Crinkles

Doris Hickok
Yield 10 dozen

6 3/4	cups flour
1/4	teaspoon salt
2	teaspoons soda
1 1/2	teaspoons cloves
1 1/2	teaspoons cinnamon
3	teaspoons ginger
2 1/4	cups vegetable shortening
3	cups brown sugar
3	eggs
3/4	cup molasses

Combine flour, salt, soda, cloves, cinnamon, and ginger.
Set aside.

Cream shortening and sugar until light and fluffy. Add eggs and
mix. Stir in molasses. Mix in dry ingredients, scraping down bowl
at least once. When well blended, turn out and press into a disk or
into logs and chill for at least 1 hour.

Preheat oven to 350 degrees.

Form into balls or cut 1/2 inch slices off logs and place on baking
sheet. Bake for 10-12 minutes. Cool on rack.

Truly Unrivaled Chocolate Chip Cookies

Janet Hickok
Yield 10 dozen

1	cup vegetable shortening
1/2	cup butter -- room temperature
1 1/2	cups sugar
1 1/2	cups brown sugar
3	large eggs
2	teaspoons vanilla
1 1/2	teaspoons salt
1 1/2	teaspoons baking soda
5 1/2	cups flour
1 1/2	cups chocolate chips -- or to taste
1 1/2	cups walnuts -- chopped, optional

Cream shortenings and sugars until light colored and fluffy. Add eggs and vanilla and beat until combined. Add soda and salt, mix. Add flour and mix well, making sure to scrape the sides so that all ingredients are combined evenly and thoroughly. Fold in chocolate chips and nuts. Chill dough for at least 40 minutes before forming into cookies.

Preheat oven to 350 degrees. Prepare baking sheets with parchment paper and set aside.
Bake for 12-15 minutes, until lightly browned and cooked just enough to take the shine off of the center of the cookie. Switch shelves half way through baking.

NOTE: Use this dough as the base for any number of add-ins

NOTE: I often roll the dough into logs and freeze so that I always have fresh baked cookies on hand. Simply let logs stand at room temperature until they are easily sliced into coins, about 15 minutes. Alternatively, you can "punch" these out with a cookie/ice cream scoop and freeze in individual pucks. Keep in mind that baking from the freezer may increase baking time by up to 1 minute. These cookies also freeze well after baking.

Real Hot Fudge Sauce

Yield Approx. 4 cups

1 1/4	**cups sugar**	
1	**cup heavy cream**	
2/3	**cup milk**	
2/3	**cup light corn syrup**	
4	**tablespoons unsalted butter -- cut into chunks**	
1/8	**teaspoon salt**	
8	**ounces unsweetened chocolate --**	
	coarsely chopped	
2 1/2	**teaspoons vanilla**	

In a large heavy saucepan stir together the sugar, heavy cream, milk, corn syrup, butter, and salt with a large wooden spoon. Bring to a boil over medium-high heat, stirring frequently and watching carefully. Reduce the heat to moderate. Rinse the spoon. Cook the caramel, stirring occasionally and gently, until the mix thickens, about 3 minutes. Continue to cook, stirring constantly and watching carefully, to prevent scorching, until the mix is a pale caramel color, about 10 minutes longer. Immediately remove the pan from the heat.

Stir the chocolate into the caramel until completely melted. Stir in 1/3 cup of hot water and the vanilla until mixed well. Set the sauce aside to cool to very warm. At this point if it is too thick, gradually thin it with more hot water until fluid but still fairly thick and gooey.

Use with the Banana Flippin Eclairs, page 176 and to top Absolutely Incredible Ice Cream, page 161.

NOTE: The sauce can be covered and chilled for up to 3 weeks. Reheat in a double boiler or in microwave at 50% power, rotating and stirring frequently.

Doriola-Snackerdoodles

Doris Hickok
Yield 10 dozen

5 1/3	**cups flour**
4	**teaspoons cream of tartar**
2	**teaspoons baking soda**
1	**teaspoon Kosher or sea salt**
4	**teaspoons cinnamon**
4	**tablespoons sugar**
2	**cups butter -- soft**
2 1/2	**cups sugar**
4	**eggs**
1	**teaspoon vanilla**

Preheat oven to 400 degrees.

Mix the flour, cream of tartar, baking soda, and salt in a medium bowl and set aside.

Mix cinnamon and sugar together and place in small bowl; set aside.

With an electric mixer, cream butter and sugar until light and fluffy, about 5 minutes on medium speed. Add eggs and mix until well blended. Stir in vanilla. Stir in the flour combination, 1/2 cup at a time, until all is well incoporated.
Chill well. Roll dough into balls and then roll into cinnamon and sugar mix and place 2 inches apart on a cookie sheet.

Bake for 10-12 minutes.

NOTE: These cookies should be light and tender and almost underbaked. They are done when the sheen is just gone and the edges are just starting to tan.

About the Author...

Janet Hickok traveled up the AlCan Highway to Alaska for the first time in 1970, in a Travel-All attached to a 30-foot trailer, along with 6 siblings and an incredibly brave Father. That was the start of many trips north, and in 1987 started work at a sport fishing lodge in the Lake Clark/Lake Iliamna area.

Janet spends half the year in Alaska working as Chef and Manager at Newhalen Lodge, and lives in Oregon during the winter months. Between trips around the country, she spends the majority of her off-season painting watercolors and, most recently, making jewelry and working in pastels.

For the past eighteen years she has lived a semi-nomadic life, never living one full year in one place. She has traveled and worked in various locales in the United States and paints whatever each particular region inspires. It is this variety of travel that is reflected in her work. "I thrive on variety and cannot and won't, limit myself to one style, medium, or locale. Where I am, what I am doing, what kind of day it is, and what mood I'm in are all reflected in my artwork. Inspiration surrounds and encompasses me no matter where I am. There is always something that begs to be painted," she explains.

Hickok's most recent works feature landscapes of the many different regions she visits annually, and also the every day still-lives particular to each region. Her artwork is in private collections across the states and abroad, as well as in galleries. She especially loves when an individual appreciates her art work enough to make a purchase, and add one of her paintings to their collection, but nothing is greater than her love of painting, and being able to paint what inspires her, and that is found abundantly in remote Alaska.

Index

Salads

Vegetables

Sweets and Goodies

About the Author...